Abstract painting

Background and American phase

Abstract painting

A Lee Ault Edition

Prepared and produced by Chanticleer Press, New York
First published by The Viking Press, Inc., in November 1951
Published on the same day in the Dominion of Canada
by the Macmillan Company of Canada Limited
Printed in U.S.A.

Thomas B. Hess

Abstract painting

Background and American phase

The Viking Press

New York 1951

Foreword

Abstract painting: Background and American phase

Abstract art has always existed, but until this century it never knew of its existence. It has become philosophies and styles, and, as such terms imply, both reflects and is in itself a way of life.

The environment that the modern world chooses to accept from behind the lens of a telescope or microscope or Leica or shutter on a Hollywood lot has been found to resemble the images of modern art. But the fact that these pictures are *actuel* should neither impress nor prejudice. Painting, although a social act, is of, not from the time—just as a tree is of a meadow, and though bent by the same wind, and growing in the same earth, sunlight, and water, still has its own roots and blossoms.

Seasonally, the death of abstract art is joyfully announced in certain high places. Its body is sometimes reported to be lying against the end-wall of a blind alley ("you can't go any further with a white rectangle"); sometimes the corpse is recognized as a suicide in a bankruptcy proceeding ("young artists haven't caught fire") or a victim of overeating ("young artists have burnt themselves out"); a few of the more imaginative members of the wake have decided to proclaim its nonexistence ("back to Cézanne!"). But seasonally, too, new abstract painters appear with unfamiliar forms, created with new ideas, deriving from living traditions. That such appearances recently have been made in America, and in fact that they constitute one of this country's major contributions to contemporary culture, is the subject of this book.

a Arshile Gorky

The Betrothal 11, 1947

b Mark Tobey

Space Intangibles, 1949, tempera

c Willem de Kooning

Collage, 1950

7

d Jackson Pollock

Number 5, 1950

8

Contents

Part one

Qualifications, propositions, contradictions, definitions

Page 10

Part two

Background and Paris

Page 28

Part three

Foreground and New York

Page 92

Part one

Qualifications, propositions, contradictions, definitions

Painting is both eye and hand and when words attempt to intercept their vision and motion they must either digress or approximate. We can wander into the fields of chronology or biography or speculate about contemporaneous sensibility, the attitudes of forgers, motives of patrons. We can try to communicate a similar response with different materials and, like a Lewis Carroll character, break into little poems of our own. Then, usually, we feel that the picture under discussion is standing by contemptuously, untouched, untroubled, and vastly unenlightened.

As soon as a painting is approached, interpretation begins: observation becomes translation, for the golden cloak of the young Botticelli is not "golden"; Mondrian's rectangles are not simple "rectangles"; even the newspaper column that Juan Gris pasted on a picture has stopped being a "newspaper column." So it is quite natural that the various problems presented by abstract painting have been discussed in an atmosphere filled with multiple-meanings, secret value judgments, and quite apparent contradictions.

A brilliant young American sculptor, David Hare, recently stated that "abstract" art is characterized by a conscious elimination of all natural forms from the image. His examples were Mondrian and the late Kandinsky, and he felt that this direction was a bad one. On the other hand, Hilla Rebay, at the time head of the Museum of Non-Objective Painting in New York, wrote that "abstract" art retains certain aspects of nature – that artists in this category created their forms in a process of *abstracting from* objects existing in the environment. Contrariwise, certain pictures by Kandinsky, or Mondrian, or

1 Pieter de Hooch

Dutch Courtyard, 1658

Abstract painting

2 Pieter de Hooch

Dutch Courtyard, 1658-59

Rudolf Bauer, because they contain only "pure" geometric shapes, cannot be called abstract. Being "*ab*" nothing (except, presumably, the music of the spheres), they should be called only "non-objective." Miss Rebay, too, equates "abstract" with something undesirable – a misguided and mongrel tendency. Both she and Hare could start off in complete agreement ("down with abstract art") and proceed from this alliance to total misunderstanding.

If we are guided by common usage, the definition in Webster's *New International Dictionary* seems fairly efficient: "Abstract, Paint. and Sculp.: Characterized by little or no reference to the appearance of objects in nature." This takes care of the "non-objective" pictures and also includes the many Picassos, Braques, Mirós, etc., which are generally included in the category.

The joker, of course, is the word "little." Just how much do you have to resemble nature before you stop being called abstract and start being called something else? But there is little profit in attempting to settle such a boundary – a sort of blundering line between bigness and littleness of resemblance. Here we must recognize that we have entered a domain of translation and approximation, and the language will make sense only as it stays relevant to the objects. Roger Fry and Clive Bell have shown, by the very honesty with which they have pursued an argument, how a trail of words, leading to inevitable conclusions, can, during the process, deny a number of painters' reputations that Clive Bell and Roger Fry might prefer to honor.

The artist, working with his eye and hand, may or may not be interested in using certain visual elements which will be recognized by the spectators as accurate reproductions. Jan van Eyck found it important to detail each bristle of hair on a man's chin, and each bristle of hair became an order of paint, a surface of form, a posi-

3 Pieter de Hooch

Courtyard of a Dutch House, 1665

4 Pieter de Hooch

Interior of a Dutch House, ca. 1660

tive statement of color. He could make the bristle symbolic of the relation of man to God, of man to his world; he gave it an infinity of meanings, but all of them refer back to paint, whose basic means of suggestion is the intangible one of exact and inevitable rightness of aspect. Van Eyck was interested in reality in the same way that Velasquez was interested in blackness or Kurt Schwitters in little torn bits of trolley-car tickets. Reality was as much a material as a bottle of linseed oil or a long-handled brush. The two oranges below the window-sill in the Arnolfini wedding picture, two bright circles almost kissing, are only perfect as oranges and circles. If an appreciative and brilliant, but only partly educated Eskimo, on a flying visit to London's National Gallery, thought they were some kind of Renaissance tennis ball, and ignored their connotations of pulpy juice, luxurious gardens, and sunshine, he would only get a fraction of the aesthetic response which can be received from this section of van Eyck's picture.

In the œuvre of Pieter de Hooch, who was also intensely preoccupied with representing the natural world, there are fascinating examples of how nature becomes artists' material (in the most commercial sense of the term). Four meticulously circumstantial images of upper middle-class life in mid-seventeenth-century Holland are reproduced here [figs. 1-4] – all of them executed by de Hooch between 1658 and 1665. Each image is complete in itself; each seems imbued with a deep, almost mystical sense of the world, of the order of life and the place of man within this order. Yet a juxtaposition of the four works (and they hang near each other in the National Gallery in London) show how little this feeling of humanism and of ethics has to do with the pictures. The serving girl at the right in the first illustration pauses as she carries a wine-filled glass into the sunny courtyard. Her form appears again

5 Second-century A.D. French

Four-headed trophy, stone

in the second picture – the pattern of her left foot, the turn of her dress, even the action of the long-nosed profile, work in almost exactly the same way. In the fourth picture she again enters from the right; the free hand drops over the apron as it does in the first picture; the profile and the lowered right hand once more announce a poised, advancing element in the picture space. Or look, in the second, third, and fourth pictures, at the rather mysterious figure – always at the left of the composition – who turns three-quarters towards the background. Her distinctive, aristocratic silhouette stands like a serene and muted sentinel which at once arrests and enriches the flow of golden light through the painting. Compare the doorways in the first and second pictures; the reversal in the pattern made by full- and half-length bricks; the introduction of white blocks over the arch in the second picture; the almost identical positions of the shutters. Note, too, in the first three, the deep openings of space at the left, and how this rhythm (which is practically a de Hooch signature) is echoed in the interior scene by a map (itself a symbol of distant space) which takes the position of the tunnel of rectangles.

These repetitions, far from suggesting lack of originality or simply a lazy system of work, actually enhance each other's beauty, giving an obsessive, mysterious, fugal power to the forms. And as we examine them attentively, they become filled with a serene, unquestioning power that is characteristic of the greatest religious art.

Perhaps Pieter de Hooch was painting religious works – his sense of the value of dignity and of the nobility of things that by constant use have acquired an existence in humanity, seems to spring from as deep a mystique as that which so agonizingly twisted the arms of Christ in the German Crucifixions of a century before. But here is a different sort of painter, and his means

6 Sixteenth-century French

Nailing of Christ to the Cross

of expressing a deep concern are more integrated with his attitude towards his life as an artist. (Also by de Hooch's time the place of the artist in the order of society was a distinct, respected one; whereas even the self-congratulating Cellini [1500-1571] kept complaining that he ought to be recognized as being better than his craftsmanship, better than this banker or that lawyer – in fact be accepted by society as one of its members with various privileges and exemptions from regulations.) De Hooch does not hesitate to switch a shape around, almost arbitrarily, from one picture to another; to change a pattern in a courtyard to fit some different relationship of actions. He retains resemblances to appearances of objects in nature, and thus, according to the dictionary definition, is no abstractionist; but then again he is, for he has created his own nature. Pictorial elements are manipulated with the identical gesture that an Ingres, a Picasso, or a de Kooning

uses to transcribe a piece of their nature from painting to painting. De Hooch is not interested in imitating the profile of a serving girl he once observed, or a lady's silhouette, but is passionately absorbed in the de Hooch profile and in the shape of the silhouette he has invented. And nature is applied to the two-dimensional surface as if it were paint. The feelings of awe and of absolute rightness which the spectator senses do not come from any recognition of moral caliber or fidelity to historically ascertainable conditions, but from the fact that these forms and this paint are one and the same, from every point of view. The mystique of logic is also that of logical tones and space. This art of an orderly society is indeed for art's sake, for only then can it be for anyone's or anything's sake.

Painters may be concerned with nature only as nature concerns observant people – as the material from which to create. But in working from

Abstract painting

this source, many have gone on to other forms – memorized, invented, or achieved intuitively – that have as little relationship to the environment which was used as have coal, water, and air to nylon. Such removals from resemblance have taken place for any number of reasons.

The stone trophy illustrated here [fig. 5] was carved in Gaul by an artist who had some dim connection with the vanishing traditions of Classical Roman sculpture. The obdurate nature of the material, his obviously unskilled hands – both kept this object from resembling four human heads. Too, the artist may not have been much concerned with representing, or with art. He wanted an image of stern, patriarchal power; he made the eyes stare by pushing them out from their sockets; the heavily jutting forms have little knowledge of skin stretched over flesh and bone. The fact that he could not get a likeness, even if he wanted to, did not prevent him from creating an effective piece of sculpture. But lack of skill does hinder, and the ancestral Frenchman who made the Aix trophy, even if he could nobly refuse a commission for some Shakespeare Garden in a benevolent park-scheme, works with a simple, dogged inspiration that suggests the dignified boredom and prim self-satisfaction characteristic of most naïve art.

The sixteenth-century French craftsman who painted the provincial image of Christ being nailed to the cross [fig. 6] knew better, and radically changed the appearance of objects in nature for reasons of his own choosing. His problem was one of space, of two spaces: the represented distance backward into the picture, from the horses' legs in the foreground, over the hill down which rides a troop of lancers, to Jerusalem about seven miles away, and on back into the infinity of blue sky. The other space is the one a spectator can touch – the measurable area from base of panel to top of panel; from side to side. In order to fix

the former within the latter, the artist used the simple principle of diminishing scale – the horsemen in the background are identified with their position at the edge of the woods by being smaller than the horsemen in the foreground. The artist thoroughly understood this device, yet he evidently felt that the figure of Christ should carry, like a magnet, its own superhuman scale. Towering over trees and cavalry is the squatting executioner at the right cross-bar. His larger role and intimacy with God gives him a giant's stature, and the artist did not stumble over, but delighted in the inconsistency, making the most of the opportunity to relish a theatrical villain. The twisting, flat shapes of the lancers' pennons at the top left – objects of no particular importance to the story of Calvary – are also fantastically out of scale, and are elaborated to give simple, violent rhythms to the upper and emptier parts of the composition. Conventions of verisimilitude are obeyed insofar as they help the creative act and its pictorial as well as narrative effects; where they interfere, they are discarded unhesitatingly.

The establishment of such conventions – linear and aerial perspective; schemes for representing anatomy two-dimensionally; foreshortening; the fixed or multiple light source; approximations of reflection, shadow, and blinding light – was achieved in periods of fanatical exploration and exultant discovery. As soon as the vanishing points that so delighted and tortured a Uccello became axioms, they interested most artists no more and no less than a new solvent for paint or a new material for brushes.

It was for no privately artistic reason, however, that the twelfth-century master who carved the capitol of *The Winds* [fig. 7] for the choir of the Abbey Church of Cluny chose to neglect the aesthetics and moralities of resemblance. His omniscience of craft is evident at a glance. A wild, grimacing figure at the corner, holding a

7 Twelfth-century French

The Winds, ca. 1120, stone

bag of wind, sinks into the fluctuating masses of stone, into deeply undercut coils of vegetation, only to re-appear, as the eye moves with the forms, in a more cheerfully menacing shape than ever. The upward and downward vectors combine with sustaining, resilient horizontals to express the capitol's position and role in a hierarchy of architecture. And the architecture haunts every cut of the chisel. Even where the sculptor could be free of structural requirements and allow himself the fullest range of expression, he insists on binding the conception to the idea of expressing the function and the place this object must occupy in the church's structure. This is not to imply that form, for some ethical reason or other, should express function – a noble, banal simplification that once threatened to change buildings into transparent toys. The Romanesque genius embraced this way of seeing and working because he also was creating the tradition while working in it, and Romanesque tradition laughed at resemblance. The leering grotesque, his flowing cloak, the canny grasp he has on the bag that will free wind through the world from his direction, remain in the stone. But the existence of the surrounding walls and vaults, the thrusts and weights which fired both sculptor and architect, set his body in a wildly unnatural position. Although the stone moved under the artist's hands as if it were some magically reinforced whipped cream, as it would for Bernini and Rodin, it was shaped according to opinions other than those of reliable optical experience.

Another road away from reality can lead away from pictorial art. Bérard and Blake [figs. 8 and 9], the humble Parisian success and the arrogant English failure, box-officewise, both departed from resemblance to intensify realist images. In his vision of Brunelleschi, Blake is fascinated by man-becoming-beast and the beast-man. He pushes urgently toward the visual realization of

Abstract painting

8 William Blake

Brunelleschi of Florence Transformed into a Serpent, ca. 1825

a conceptual abstraction – towards "wrong" or "evil" that can be apprehended easily. Reality of appearance is avoided only in order to convince us of the truth of the artist's moral convictions. Yet, somehow, the irrational intensity of belief in the vision, the consistent high level of awkwardness of Blake's hand, and, most of all, the straight, common-sense attitude of his illustrative approach, keep this watercolor from becoming just a tract on a liberal's ideas about Dante.

Bérard's distortions, too, seem to suggest literary, unprofessional motives. The light ocher body bending against a cerulean sky differs from conventional anatomy simply to bend more interestingly, but the placid, dedicated approach to painting – an act which Bérard modestly tried to avoid most of his life – keeps *Acrobat* from being a pretentious failure. Like Blake's illustration, and like some of Leonardo da Vinci's pictures, it is completely saturated in a distinct humanity.

We look for the picture, but keep meeting the artist, and so, before long, we are almost forced to forget the flimsiness of the former. But not all artists are Leonardo, or Blake, or even Christian Bérard. So we arrive at one of the neglected aspects of the visual arts – the bad picture.

No human being ever knelt on the ground, from no matter what exigency of ecstasy or discomfort, as do the figures of Mary Magdalen in the paintings reproduced here by Henner and Quentin Massys [figs. 10 and 11]. Distortions of anatomy are obvious in both cases. Yet examining the former, one finds the artist leaving resemblance not only in order to cheat the eye into believing that resemblance has never been left at all, a perfectly proper painter's device, but also quickly to excite a mood of pathos and pitiful sentiment. The exaggerated upper lip and neck, the abandonment of anatomically correct contours in the arms and legs, produce forms

9 Christian Bérard

Acrobat, ca. 1930

without interior consistency – they appear to have been brought together only to express Henner's idea of sensual grief. The body is schematized in the most conventional way; the pose and facial expression are simply clichés of gesture which easily can be recognized by the spectator, for the artist is working only in the tradition of the spectator's everyday perceptions, and he relies wholly upon them. The audience is asked to do the creative work. It alone can give the proper emotional content to these loosely modelled hands and sunken eyes; supply the correct interpretation to each item as it is presented by the impresario-artist. In arranging forms to be read quickly and without difficulty, Henner surrendered the main channels of aesthetic communication – and he also guaranteed a short life to his reputation by making it wholly contemporaneous. His not inconsiderable talent accepted the job of evoking immediate verbal responses,

which, in turn, would poke the glands that start tears or produce less respectable symptoms of passion. But whatever glands there are that function more or less directly from the stimulus of a work of art, he could rarely excite.

The Massys, on the other hand, seems completely successful as a picture, and thus successful as Mary Magdalen, for we recognize the lady in the Henner to be but an attractive, indiscreet, and possibly devout girl. One can examine the Flemish Renaissance Mary from innumerable interpretive approaches. But if one starts with the shapes – looking, for instance, at the triangular spaces made by the sky behind the hill and tree, by the figure's arms, by the plot of grass to the right, by the space between the hip and ankle and that between the jar and its cover – one finds a whole, interlocked mechanism of solids and voids, of darks and lights, which to some may suggest the soaring, spinning forms of a Gothic

10 Jean Jacques Henner

Mary Magdalen at the Tomb of Christ, ca. 1890

cathedral, to others a more Freudian meaning, to still others a fusion of gesture with figure with landscape. Here everything leads simultaneously to and from form toward the total effect of the work of art. And the spectator will bring from the picture far more than he brings to it.

If the Massys, by a coincidence of subject, is useful as a way to underline the weakness of the Henner, the latter should not be dismissed in recognizing the former's greatness, for it has been truly pointed out that we do not look at bad pictures enough.

There are many qualities that one could praise in Henner's Magdalen: it is original as far as subject matter and style are concerned; it is also traditional in that it observes certain conventions of figure painting which had been honored by many of the greatest Neo-Classical and Romantic masters. One could mention such painters as Crespi, or Delacroix, or Courbet in discussing its various aspects, yet anyone who has had the briefest introduction to Henner's œuvre could attribute this Magdalen to his hand. Thus there is an individuality present, and, too, it cannot be disparaged simply because it is communicating easily with fellow humans. One may like or dislike the work, but it cannot puzzle, much less mystify. Still, as the picture seems wholly unsuccessful, what does such praise mean? All these verbal virtues seem irrelevant to the aesthetic quality, and become, as far as painting is concerned, more or less suspect. Especially suspicious becomes the praise of originality, for though Henner might have been able to "talk" his picture in such a way that anyone might admit it to be an interestingly new notion, still this concept of novelty seems to be a stereotype of the most dangerous kind – comparable in art, perhaps, to the American convention of "success."

In the bad picture often will be found the product of an artist – whether he has left resem-

11 Quentin Massys

Mary Magdalen, ca. 1510

blance or fights towards it – who has stopped thinking about painting. He may be thoughtlessly repeating, over and over again, a masterpiece he once made; he may be honestly trying to make an honest dollar; or courageously exploring the unknown territories of his subconscious, or the salons of high society. But all eyes (the spectators' as well as the artist's) have left the painting.

Some artists, in order to heighten a certain idea of reality, have left resemblance and have, indeed, looked toward the idea of an abstract art – for, perhaps, in the twentieth-century sense of the term, abstractness does not depend so much upon degree of fidelity to nature as it does upon an *état-d'âme,* an inner compulsion to leave the appearance of the subject, instead of burrowing within it, as did a Louis LeNain or a Vermeer (which does not, of course, contradict the Webster definition previously offered, for the modern *état d'âme* produces works which the definition efficiently describes). Painters in the past, little interested in making ideologies visible, have swept their art away from any reflection of a chosen image for a number of reasons. For some, expression became involved in various relationships between pure elements of form – and one of the greatest of these was Saenredam. This seventeenth-century Hollander (and it is most apt that his twentieth-century compatriots should be Mondrian, van Doesburg, and de Kooning) was no influential exploiter of new subjects or technical variations, but in his modest way he was a triumphantly daring painter. White space, empty or solid – every sort of white, ten thousand whites – is locked into one of his masterpieces, *Interior of St. Bavo, Haarlem* [fig. 12]. The perspective is often purposefully ambiguous; arches will seem to fluctuate back and forth from wall to arcade; receding diagonals are apt

Abstract painting

12 Pieter Saenredam

Interior of St. Bavo, Haarlem, ca. 1660

to skip the eye forward as they converge on the sun-filled background. Tilting squares dance through the picture, becoming broken by massive bases of columns, echoed in the pointed vaults, and rising, without drama or ado, to the skies beyond the windows, only to drop down again into the complex mechanism of constantly changing intervals. The vast nave of St. Bavo becomes paper-thin, and still it can expand to vaster dimensions than it ever had as tensions between conventions of depth and the subtle balances of hue and form make themselves felt. But, of course, Saenredam is not de Kooning, and the drama has no intention of moving on to this stage. Although a crucial ambiguity remains, St. Bavo wins, as Saenredam wanted it to win all along. Still, the artist discovered these hard, chalky lines and arcs, and they, too, become his subject even as they describe the existence of a house of God.

But we must return (for the last time) to the bad painting, for the idea of using "pure shapes" can become a sort of theurgy even though these shapes, as such, have no magic to command the appearance of art.

J. Goldsborough Bruff, one of an enormous school of mid-nineteenth-century American super-realist painters, might have been aiming at "cheating the eye" in his *The Rack* [fig. 13]. But despite this fashionable motive, it seems obvious that he was also concerned with the interrelationship between certain fixed rectangles, all of which carry very exact references within the larger rectangle of the painting – the whole construction being kept quite flat by simulating a "real" wood background. The envelope, the cards, the little map, fall around the ribbon that attempts to stick them in place, like packages tumbling from the arms of a Christmas shopper. The artist appears to have been too interested in form as shape;

13 J. Goldsborough Bruff

The Rack, ca. 1845

pictorially, he is too abstract. Elements of reality (as Saenredam's elements are all realist) were not given the correct body, or were not placed in the correct fields of force to sustain the various handwritings, sketches, postal cancellations, or even the inventive six-time repetition of the artist's name. Imagine that on top of the drawing of the painter at work (near the upper left-hand corner) one glued a photostat of the *Victory of Samothrace*, flying off to the left. Would this balance the slipping insignia below and pull the king of clubs back to the pattern? But one could vary the picture endlessly, and, perhaps, just here lies its small greatness. For Bruff's cavalier attitude toward form itself produced ingratiating eccentricities.

By its very failure, however, Bruff's picture emphasizes a basic characteristic of form – it is apt to retain a certain magnetic charge of reality, whether immediately apparent or mysteriously hidden. A rectangle set on its southwest-northeast axis, if, like Bruff's, it is a map of Washington, D.C., will not necessarily appear to be set at 45 degrees (leaving out, for argument's sake, all possibility of optical illusion). From a chemical analysis of the surface to the most hidden, subconscious associations that may reach the spectator, every possible meaning of form will affect its definition in the picture. Bruff's failure came from his leaving reality before he understood its powers.

For the strange, late Gothic genius of Altdorfer, forms of pattern had the same wonderful fascination that those of space had for Saenredam. His *St. George and the Dragon in a Woody Landscape* [fig. 14] has been interpreted* as an almost mystical embodiment of the age-old forest fears that still lurked in the German mind in the early sixteenth century. But this menacing

---

*
By Sir Kenneth Clark in *Landscape Painting*.

14 Albrecht Altdorfer

St. George and the Dragon in a Woody Landscape,
1510

flood of landscape seems to have been summoned into the picture for other reasons as well. The endlessly piling-up strokes of the brush, as they describe leaves and branches, by their very accumulation destroy resemblance, and change the forest of nature into a new forest of paint. The colors and directional patterns move in and out of reality until, after having satisfied ourselves that the tiny warrior, his horse, and his defeated dragon exist, then even these necessary images melt imperceptibly into ever slower and larger masses of flickering strokes. Finally, just as a jungle can eat up a clearing, pattern triumphs over the forest itself; our eyes, entranced, dance along the shapes of leaves, trunks, or plumed helmet, aware of nothing but the rhythms of the dance. But this cannot last, for, like St. Bavo, St. George is a foregone victor, not only over his traditional adversary, but also over the patterns that so dazzled the spectator, and the artist. Then we come back to the forest, to its fearsome dominance. And, perhaps, our very experience of having been trapped within it, of having forgotten its existence within its maze, is the perfect reinforcement of Altdorfer's metaphor. Pattern may have existed for him as the supreme reality – the idea of a path of motion now whipping into recesses of darks, now turning lazily in areas of sunlit hue – may have recalled memories of the forest nightmare to his consciousness. But the Gothic painter, and the Renaissance one, for Altdorfer was both, insists on the real urgency of his dream.

A number of contemporary aestheticians (with such painters as Mondrian or Rothko in mind) would claim that if Altdorfer had forgotten the forest, forgotten St. George, forgotten everything but the hypnotic play of his brush over the picture's surface, he would have produced something which could no longer be called "art," but only "decoration." Somehow, they claim, when

15 Fifteenth-century Burgundian

Rock crystal bowl

the cord between subject (in nature) and object (created by the artist) is broken (in the mind of the spectator) then the vital forces that inform the creative act cease to operate, and the result can be only "very pretty," like a lamp in good taste or a carpet.

The logic behind such a conclusion is not impressive, for if we know anything at all about what makes us enjoy a painting, it is that it has nothing to do with its species of subject, the accuracy with which this subject is represented, or the moral, political, or subconscious motive of the artist. A masterpiece may be a sympathetic portrayal of an act that everyone abhors; its representation may be inaccurate in fact (an introduction of camels into a scene where it is known no camels could have been) or in act (a man may be depicted as having eighteen heads); finally, the artist's particular reason for executing a picture may be lamentable to decent-thinking people. Indeed, if we pushed such reasoning to its conclusions, we would have to decide that the appearance of, and resemblance to nature in a work of pictorial art can have nothing to do with its aesthetic value, except, possibly, to act detrimentally. Nature would seem to be an extraneous element, and maybe it would be best to do away with it altogether, and then work towards the evocation of a "pure" aesthetic response that logic suggests might exist.

But if these aestheticians have not been sound logicians, they have been better observers. In examining the history of art it does seem that certain images are little more than pretty, and do not involve the spectator or the artist in any experience beyond the immediate pleasures of superficial apprehension. In many of such works the ties to resemblance are weak or non-existent. Rugs, mosaics, tiles, certain tapestry designs by, say, Boucher, or many of the Romanesque frescoes, confront one with an extremely skilled art

Abstract painting

16 Titian

A Nymph and a Shepherd, ca. 1565, detail

which, nonetheless, never seems to approach the areas in which a Rembrandt, a Titian, or a Velasquez succeed or fail. However in discovering such a category, the aestheticians may have been too quick to account for it and too slow to characterize it. (Again it is. a matter of words taking flight into their own logic upon glancing contact with a visual fact.) Those works which are generally accepted as being decorative have certain family resemblances: they exploit existing ideas of form rather than invent new ones; they work with and for a cultivated or otherwise informed audience which demands distraction and delectation during periods of relaxation, or pomp during ceremony; they are continually tempted by the nuances that suggest luxury and refinement or the almost-invisible embellishment that will be appreciated by the spectator in the know, whether he be a peasant, a king, or a cardinal; relaxed, clear, and poised, they avoid

mystery, ambiguity, and revelations of intensity.

Thus, on the whole, the aestheticians are right – as observers. There is weakness, if only in the act of equating greatness with vulgarity. Nonetheless, the proposition of either some nature or no art does not seem to follow. The cutting of the umbilical cord between recognizable environment and image, which characterizes so much decorative art, has not always proved disastrous. Anyone who has seen the great Oriental and Near Eastern textiles, or Roman mosaics, or late Gothic crystals [fig. 15] would admit, I believe, than an intense, disturbing expression – without the faintest appeal to the shapes of nature – can involve the spectator just as deeply and as mysteriously as do the enigmatic demiurges of the Italian Renaissance. In lieu of the whole complexity of interpreting some livable situation, one's associative faculties are stimulated and offered an endless play of symbol and meaning.

This curlique may be a stylized dragon; that diagonal an ideograph of flight, but even without any iconological analysis, all the possibilities for fascination are offered by the (admittedly few) triumphs of such objets-d'art.

Preoccupation with (perhaps a better term would be "love of") form or pattern, as typified by Saenredam and Altdorfer, have always existed, but there is still another passion that is relevant to a discussion of abstract art – the passion for paint. In literature, excessive love of words, of their sounds and sizes, can become an unfortunate narcissist obsession, as it did for a Swinburne or a de Banville. Yet the "natural" painter seems to run no such risk when he gives himself up to the tricks of his trade. In the detail from Titian's late painting, *A Nymph and a Shepherd* [fig. 16], the thin, sticky flecks and streaks of pigment weave into a surface which is never so much sky, tree, deer, or hand as it is an overwhelming affirmation of the existence of the artist's material. The individual shape; the form that must carry the whole meaning of its component hues, lines, and masses; the repeating rhythms, gestures, and motions across and into the flat surface of the canvas, all the picture's elements seem absorbed into the beauty that Titian created as his loaded brush came in contact with the smooth, dusty-toned surface of the canvas. The work of art tends to become independent of references to anything except to its physical existence. It is irrelevant, for instance, to call a certain passage clumsy or a section of the composition awkward. Such criticism, although quite reasonable, ceases to have meaning when confronted with the spectacularly rich surface which Titian prepared for the eye. Almost condescendingly, the artist offers his vision of nature – which is unbelievably impressive, astonishing, and intricate – for, towering above any tree or sky (or line or shape or interval of space) is the all-engrossing drama of Titian painting.

If one looks at a Watteau for what one has appreciated in a Matisse, one can lose Watteau, just as one could lose "Lycidas", reading it within the reference of an appreciation for "Dry Salvages." Calling an old picture "modern" may indicate that it is forgotten for the memory of a different experience. But the accepted past, which is a sanctuary for common praise, can inform the inevitably controversial present, and, like a lawyer's line of questions in examining a witness, lay a foundation for the acceptance of new evidence. The past itself stays serene, changeless and changing, offering new aspects of its condition to each generation, but retaining all aspects intact within itself.

For present painting, the past can testify to the fact that no art is abstract, for genius can invest any form, no matter how capriciously invented, with an intensity that will make it concrete to all understanding observers; too, all art is abstract in that it is away from its subject's original syndrome in nature – different from everyday experience, in fact "ab" nature "in" art.

Thus "abstract" art can become just a familiar phrase of identification, as the term "skyscraper" is a convenient tag for certain buildings. If "abstract" pictures have in common all those aesthetic characteristics with which we are familiar throughout the history of art, they are nonetheless tremendously different from the paintings of the immediate past – just as Giotto's three-dimensional anatomies were different from the paper-thin bodies of Cavallini's heroes. Being of a new century, they offer new problems and new satisfactions. All that the past should do for the present is to affirm its right to modernity – and to preserve magnificent proofs of the existence of greatness in the visual arts.

Part two

Background and Paris

Listen to me! I am the gullet of Paris
And if I feel like it, I'll drink the universe . . .
Guillaume Apollinaire, *Vendémaire*

The history of art is like a kaleidoscope, the late professor Henri Focillon said. With sufficient hindsight, one can gather the parts together, then examine them through the eyepiece and admire the handsome, symmetrical design they produce. But hand the mechanism to someone else to look at, or give it a tap, and the same parts fall into a completely changed, just as orderly, pattern. Perhaps in different images certain parts will play roles of different importance – in fact it may happen that, as time goes on, some pieces will be lost or some previously unnoticed ones rediscovered – but on the whole the components will remain much the same, despite their endlessly changing relationships.

The logical, affirmative development of abstract art from the styles of the past has been described efficiently and brilliantly over and over again. There is little need to retrace here the steps that now seem to have led so inexorably from Ingres' inspired Neo-Classicism and formal inventions to the Post-Impressionists' "wild-beast" streaks of pigment. But in this dramatic development – which is also the story of one of the most lavishly creative periods ever known in the history of painting – and in the subsequent flowering from it of the bewildering maze of contemporary "isms,"* modern American abstract paint-

Viz. Intimism, Fauvism, Expressionism, Cubism, Futurism, Orphism, Synchronism, Neoplasticism, Suprematism, Constructivism, Non-Objectivism, Elementaryism, Vorticism, Rayonnism, Dadaism, Surrealism, Neo-Romanticism, to say

17 Paul Cézanne

Victor Choquet, 1877

18 Pablo Picasso

M. Uhde, 1910

ing has its roots. So it becomes important to seek the angle of the kaleidoscope that will set art history in a position to present the best possible view of this particular past. Perhaps some of the more important pieces will be but partially visible in the process, and some rather minor ones may tend to assume major positions. I hope that this will be excused on the grounds that we are not looking for justifications, but are only engaged in an effort to admire the ancestry of our present.

The action will take place in France, Russia, Central Europe, Holland, Italy, England, and America. But nationalities will tend to become indistinct – to blend with each other – and the individual attitude towards nation will be that of the self-confident cosmopolitan. Still, the locale will be important, for no matter where the action takes place, the backdrop is reminiscent of Paris – where the main plot of this history is laid.

Chronology will have a comparatively minor role. There has been much to-do lately about who did what when; who got the idea; who followed and who lead, with little medals for "firstness" distributed to each victor. An art critic happily will dig up some rather ineffectual drawings and, pointing at the date, 1904, claim that it was here Cubism began. Even a few artists, rather touchingly, have forged backward the dates of some of their paintings – as if they were so unsure of the work's aesthetic merit that they had to place all trust in the dubious claims of historical significance. But in this backward look, we are more concerned with the completed statement than its evolution – it is more a matter of how a style arrived than who started it.

In the first group of illustrations [figs. 17 to 23], the human figure seems to go through a meta-

nothing of such terms which do not lend themselves very handily to suffixes, like The Bridge, The Blue Rider, The Metaphysical School, De Stijl, Proun, Merz, as well as such dubious appellations as Neo-Primitivism, Intrasubjectivism, Tubism, etc., etc.

morphosis of crystallization and release, and the play-acting drama of recognizable expression becomes more and more subordinate to a new hero, who is motivated by the artists' creative action.

In Cézanne's portrait [fig. 17], 1877, the likeness of his friend and early patron, Victor Choquet, seems to swim behind lumps and flecks of densely manipulated pigment. It is as if a face has been frozen in an icy substance; one cannot tell exactly which is face and which is ice. Cézanne had taken the idea of little strokes of paint from the revolutionary methods inaugurated by Pissarro and Monet. Searching for a way with which to capture the effects of light on the surface of their canvases, these Impressionists evolved a manner of dissolving a form into arbitrary* units of color, building the façade of a cathedral or a humble vegetable garden with an infinity of tiny areas of hue, which, in turn, were expected to blend, as the spectator moved away from the picture, into the play of sun and shadow across the image. But a spectator seldom stays twenty feet away from the object he is looking at, and, contrary to popular belief, many of these Impressionist works do not blend at all, but remain flat, granular surfaces in which the construction of bumpy hatches can never be overlooked. From their work, Cézanne adopted the prophetic ideas that each part of the picture can be brought to a finish of equal importance (no more vague, receding backgrounds which will let a face or a mountain drop in one's lap); that by breaking up the surface of the painting with an increasingly complicated texture, the drama will be pulled back into its own two-dimensional

*

Working within their reverent attitudes toward nature, neither Monet nor Pissarro would have accepted this adjective, but would have claimed that each purple or crimson streak had been observed in the motif. Yet despite all programs, both enthusiastically went beyond such observations to an "arbitrary" exploitation of intense color for its own sake.

existence (no more framed holes in the wall); and, finally, by insisting upon the importance of the painting as a painting, Monet and Pissarro seemed to be breaking free from the ideas of decoration and imitation which had been increasingly burdensome to artists in that period when public and official taste were attracted to the most vulgar sorts of sentimental virtuosity.

Monet and Pissarro were revolutionary in method, and even pushed their methods to the point where it was sometimes practically impossible for them to create successful paintings. In giving the image a new existence – in endowing it with the means of independent communication with the spectator – they also tended to make painting a simple act of glorification of this liberty. It was Cézanne who undertook the possibly reactionary task of giving bounds to the Impressionists' freedom, of filling it with his own fanatical sense of structure and order, and, as he said, of making it an art of the museums.

It is not a matter of finding some pleasing hierarchy of forms in M. Choquet's features or of discovering a Platonic beauty in the relationship of a triangular nose to a triangular hairline to some supreme state of "triangleness." Cézanne recognized that M. Choquet's face, as a face, was perfect, as God and M. Choquet had made it. But to make a painting which would resemble it, to give some idea of the personality that it expressed as well as the painter's attitude toward it, and still fulfill the artist's new and stringent demands for the ordered independence of pictorial art, became the engrossing and never-ending problem. Its solution is one of Cézanne's eternal glories.

By breaking up the surface, by making each section of paint insist upon its place in the visible scheme, the artist exalts the two-dimensionality of his work. In building up and inter-relating the colors and in the most meticulous refinement of the interlocking forms, he also arrives at a means

Abstract painting

19 Georges Braque

Man with a Guitar, 1911

of showing the nose's advance in front of the cheek, but still reversing this forward jut by powerful backward pushes as a contour twists off its anatomical direction towards another position in space, or as a warm yellow in front identifies itself with an identical tone behind. Such tension between object and surface is exactly what we have seen in Saenredam and Titian, but with Cézanne tension is not disguised. He almost never assumed the old masters' perfected mask – that of ease of execution. In fact, of all great painters he proclaims his clumsiness the loudest – which is, of course, another, but rather less efficient disguise. As soon as tension is revealed, the inner mechanism of order assumes a major role. The artist will show us how he could get the neck to fit with the shirt; how he finally found a way to make his sitter's passively sympathetic expression (Cézanne's models always look slightly honored and as if they had been holding the pose a terribly long time – which they had) work with the very subtle horizontal arc of left eye, bridge of nose, right eye, ear, and background. When the cheekbone arrived at its angular definition in the picture space, the artist could easily have gone on a bit further and smoothed it over. But Cézanne must always take us behind the scenery and proudly display the intricate machinery he has devised; he carefully hides a few makeshift patches. In this eloquent gesture at his genius he begins the story of modern abstract painting.

Assuming the value of the Cézanne, one could plead for recognition of Picasso's portrait [fig. 18] 1910, and Braque's *Man with a Guitar* [fig. 19], 1911, but this would not only be gross oversimplification, but also involve serious errors. It is evident that the faceted planes of Cézanne can be recognized in an exaggerated form in the Cubist paintings; too, the grandiloquent display of structure, so revolutionary in the older master's work, is also made here; and it is well known that a close study of Cézanne's art strongly influenced – if not actually made possible – the development of the whole Cubist movement. But such continuous-heritage presentations (Fragonard comes out of Boucher; Giotto from Cimabue) invariably dilute their subject, except when an artist did make himself a sort of fabulous son of his master – as van Dyck did of Rubens, or as Lancret did of Watteau.

Picasso's portrait of his friend, Wilhelm Uhde, the perspicacious dealer-collector and promoter of primitive painting, is from one point of view as backward-looking in terms of Cézanne's portrait as Cézanne's is in terms of Monet and Pissarro. The adjustment of form, the systematically displayed mechanism of space, are made to help capture recognizable reality as well as to flex magnificent painter's muscles before the spectator. But Picasso is so deeply involved in the appearance of his subject that he distorts this appearance to give its impact added force. Seen from one angle, as Titian would have painted it, Uhde's face would be incomplete, and our knowledge of it would be fragmentary – just as we only know one side of the moon. Picasso will show us the eyes in profile and head on; we see the silhouette of the nose as it turns before us; the whole bone-structure of the head fascinated this Spanish Parisian, and he elaborated it with the virtuosity of a great anatomist. This curious process of sacrificing reality in order to enter more deeply into it will be examined at greater length in a discussion of collages, but it is still worth noting here that from his familiarity with the portrait, its owner, Roland Penrose, was able to recognize Uhde – whom he had never met – many years later as that gentleman happened to walk by a café terrace.

Behind, in front of, and transfiguring the likeness of Uhde, however, are the shattered and rearranged geometries of a table, a wall, a coat, a drawer. The construction of the painting dominates, even though the material from which it was made (that is, the real table, wall, coat, drawer, etc.) continues to haunt every sharpened angle. The painted image of Uhde is swallowed by the flood of his painted environment, and the V-shape of his upper lip goes echoing endlessly throughout the picture; the process of echoing becomes as important as the represented lip.

The Cubists' fragmentation and re-assembly of reality are seen more clearly and consistently in the Braque, for this Frenchman has little madness. Where the genius of Picasso would endlessly glorify the very element it was destroying, the more conventional talent of Georges Braque simply pushed along the given direction as thoroughly, sensitively, and as brilliantly as possible. (In this respect Braque is a great conventional painter and his fortunate destiny was that he happened to be at the proper time and place to help establish the convention that would satisfy him for the rest of his life.) The game of figuring out where are the man and the guitar in this picture can be a fascinating one, just as it is wonderful to see some scholarly iconologist unravel the significance of a Mantegna allegory. But it is perhaps even less important, for if Mantegna was not too concerned with just which attributes are proper to each demi-divinity, at least he entered into the game and followed the Humanists as far as he could. Braque's concern with the musician and his instrument is only as an accepted and singularly apt bundle of motifs. Clefs, scrolls, fretwork, fingers, head, shoulders, all become a source for arcs which, rising and falling, settle into rectangles, until, accompanied by the last fading notes of their prior existence in the center of the image, they blend into the final solid rectangle that bounds the canvas. The artist takes the revealed construction of Cézanne, and, in a process of refinement and embellishment, returns it to the great French tradition of decorative painting.

Abstract painting

20 Marc Chagall

Half-Past Three, 1911

The misanthropic old master of Aix, with furious labor (the legend is that the trees outside Cézanne's studio were sometimes festooned with canvases which the dissatisfied and enraged artist had skimmed out of his window), dug up the bones of painting which for centuries had been politely covered; Braque almost immediately enshrined them as relics so that they could reassume their role in the procession of fashion.

His chosen subject, a guitar player, is most apt, as is Chagall's gentleman smoking a cigarette, writing in a garden, at *Half-Past Three* [fig. 20], 1911. The art of the early Cubists reflects the life of a leisurely, decorous bohemia which evidently foresaw an untroubled and steadily more successful future. Picasso and the Futurists may have been loyal to the program of misunderstood rebellion, and savage indignation often bursts from their calmest compositions, but, on the whole, the climate in Paris, pre-World War I, was fair and brisk; the nineteenth-century's optimistic dream still perfumed the air.* The universe was contained; the body of knowledge, ever enlarging; knowledge was wisdom. Still more important for the painter in Paris, he had behind him a record of triumphant, rugged individualism that went back, without a break, to David and Delacroix. It was accepted that each generation would certainly discover a world for itself. In the beginning, of course, an ironclad bourgeoisie would scream with dismay and attack, through semi-slapstick critics, any attempt to shock the public into seeing differently. But each generation was also bound to produce its geniuses, its sympathetic intellectual friends, and, in the end, they would win. After a few decades, the shy figure of the President of the Republic of France

*

The aroma lasted: in one of Mondrian's statement., two years before Hitler, the artist still trusted in the vision of an endless parade of humanity marching steadily toward the finite goal of peace and beauty.

might stroll in wonder through unfamiliar lands which the artists had by now colonized; probably he would offer in return for this tangible evidence of glory the ribbon of the Legion of Honor (which the painter might grandly refuse). The role of the bourgeois was as stereotyped as that of the genius, and the amazing thing is that the geniuses had always appeared. In 1910, there was no particular reason to suppose that they would not keep coming on indefinitely.

The artists, with their poet-friends, their wives, mistresses, admirers, were a society. Some, like Gris, worked long, regular hours; a Modigliani burned himself out in a glamorous flash of love, talent, and lyricism; one painter might be so poverty-stricken that months would be wasted in the crushingly grim routine of keeping alive; others, approaching middle-age, were already entering the vestibule of the palace of success. And it was a palace, for success was not suspect – it was either a ridiculous, short-lived joke or a well-earned reward. Spaniards, Russians, Italians, Englishmen, American, Hungarians – every nationality and race could gain a new identity within this society which seemed to offer the privileges and the tragedies of anarchy, but which, in retrospect, appears to have had many more conforming tribal characteristics than might have been noticed at the time. If ever conditions were excellent for a free passage of ideas from artist to artist, from painter to sculptor to poet to philosopher, they existed in prewar Paris.

The pictures by Braque and Chagall both exude optimistic, lighthearted energy. The Frenchman turns the shapes of his guitarist over and over, like an expert jeweler displaying some rare diamond to a discerning client. Chagall – and *Three O'clock* is an atypical work, for this Russian prodigy took from Cubism only those means with which he could intensify the affable dreams of a Chassidic Aesop – topples his frag-

ments of anatomy into diagonally moving planes, with a rose and a face and a cat all good-naturedly out of joint, to help communicate the sensations of a buoyant, garrulous temperament.

Picasso, Braque, Chagall, all of them – friends, strangers, acquaintances, enemies – must have had a feeling of having "gone beyond," of having seen that the break with reality, almost made by the Post-Impressionists, had released them into a world where painting would at the same time return to its purest state of vital, direct expression, and still carry with it all the recondite baggage of a thousand years of culture. With this power they were able to ransack museums. Before them Gauguin had gone to the primitive carvings of Breton peasants and to South Sea Edens; the Impressionists had felt what now seems to be an almost naïve shock of joy in front of Japanese woodcuts. But in the first decade of this century all the history of art – and much of it had been requisitioned by archeologists – was suddenly tumbled by the artists over their own heads. Negro African sculpture – which early had been the subject of impressive exhibitions in Germany, profoundly influencing the Expressionists – the archaic figures of Greece, Crete, Egypt, the Etruscans; paintings of children, Carolingian jewelry, Early Christian reliefs, all seemed to inform the pioneering abstractionists who discovered ancestors who were also brothers.

It is easy to overemphasize the influence such rediscovered arts had upon twentieth-century painting. Picasso certainly recognized that African sculptors had treated the plane of a cheek moving behind a nose in a way that he was about to approach. When he arrived at this manner, he had no reason not to allude to his source gratefully and learnedly, and, indeed, in many works of this period it is evident that the artists decided to be influenced by certain objects they had studied in museums. But to claim that such de-

Abstract painting

liberate borrowings from primitive and archaic art were anything more than an appreciative recognition of new source material is to underestimate the artists' actions and their products. Painters, unlike such accomplished commentators as André Malraux, are seldom visual gourmets, and they will find just what they are looking for. They do not happen upon wonderful objects which will open their eyes; on the contrary, they discover them when they are quite ready to make discoveries. The art historian has long ago taken over the artists' explorations in many of these fields, and today one is as apt to see a news photograph, cut from a magazine, as a print of the tympanum of Moissac pinned to the wall of a studio. But the excitement of adventures in museums, of travels through their long-neglected departments, must have been almost as great as the excitement of a Braque who, entering Cubism, suddenly found himself at home.

With Léger and Matisse we return to more complicated and important problems – return to impacts of genius upon style similar to those of Cézanne and Picasso. Léger takes the dissecting machine of Cubism (perhaps he had as much to do in inventing it as anyone else) and adapts it to his own pictorial metaphor. Picasso, who is justly famous as the Daedalus of modern painting and sculpture, has almost invariably felt impelled to work his variations and exploitations upon the great, old subjects of painting – the seated woman with accessories and attributes; the still-life; studio interior – men and women, fighting, loving, and relaxing, as they did for Rubens or Goya. Léger, however, with a Frenchman's enthusiastic optimism and love of actuality, looked outward and took the whole newly mechanized world for his source material. He found in the machine what de Hooch had found in the Dutch courtyard – an inexhaustible source of forms which could keep their own strength of symbol and emotion as they

relate to the environment, and could also be transcribed in the non-verbal handwriting of the painter's brush.

In *The Balcony* [fig. 21], 1914, we are immediately confronted with the construction of a painting – just as we were in the portrait of M. Choquet. The artist is willing to rejoice publicly in his act of creation – one almost hears him laughing at the passage that came off so easily and so well, or ferociously working out his problems. Note the diagonals leading into the composition from the left and right edges; the ascending-screw action at the bottom; the tumbling ovals at the top. One might find almost identical schemes in a Raphael or a Dürer but it would take hours to perceive them under ingenious coverings of static details and counter-motions. But then, in exposing his action as an artist, Léger also can make it more and more complex. He invents and elaborates construction, insists on every minute thrust in the scaffolding, and finally gives a mysterious and endlessly interpretable variety to what was once a basic framework. The forms have their own ambiguities. Cylinders, ramps, and cubes are fitted together into clanging figures – awkward, athletic robots whose anatomies continually refer to the cannon and the lathe. But in performing the essentially literary act of mechanizing the countryside and its population, Léger uses this machine-metaphor as an end to a means. Highlights are arbitrarily distributed, yet such reference to modelling is never completed; bare canvas intercepts the passage that could make the rounded coil suddenly become a three-dimensional curve. Perspective, too, becomes an arbitrary stenographic notation, producing an illusion of volume that quickly is denied by a systematically contradictory set of vanishing points. Indeed, one can say that while Picasso diminished resemblance in order to increase reality, Léger adduced resemblances in order to heighten

21 Fernand Léger

The Balcony, 1914

Abstract painting

the effects of abstraction. To an iconologist, the sophisticated Spaniard may be a teller of myths; the Frenchman a fashioner of naïve emblems. But for both, the hero of the painter's act is the fabulous artificer, and his miracle is in adjusting the continually interpretable images of nature to the impetuous strategems of his art.

The final evolution of Cubism from a pioneering group into a great international style is evident in architectural pictures by Matisse and Picasso [figs. 22 and 23].

In 1916 Matisse was already an old master. He had taken the dots and colors of the late nineteenth century and with them had set off an explosion of good taste – a phenomenon characteristic of, and only of, the French genius. He must have approached Cubism with something of the attitude of a famous general taking over a new, but temporary command. He is willing to understand the local regulations and traditions; still there is never any doubt that he is strictly on his own. *The Moroccans* [fig. 22], 1916, a vast work which somehow always adjusts its scale to small reproductions – perhaps because its sweepingly brushed colors are so vital to its monumentality – at once totally ignores the past examples of Cubism and predicts its evolution for the next forty years. Matisse adopts the notions of flat space and unrecognizable object – the latter an extremely infrequent phenomenon in his œuvre. Figures, heads, domes, railings, all flip out of their context of pure shape to jab at our associations and then snap back to their ordained positions as structural parts. This is not to imply that Matisse or the Cubists in general were strict disciplinarians – a notion both inaccurate and widespread. The style, like all others, assumes various inner and outer obediences by the artist to his aims, and, indeed, for a brief while the Cubists attempted to make inner disciplines as evident as they made the inner constructions of their pic-

tures. But they were as delighted by the happy accident or sudden inspiration as a Turner or a Renoir. More important, Matisse appropriates the inner-outer actions of planes, the backward acting forward, the diagonal assuming straightness, the background becoming as important as the foreground, which had been so characteristic of Picasso and Braque in the immediately preceding years. In this prophetic picture, he goes on to exalt the very elements of Cubism that he was so soon to renounce. The dark background in the upper center of the painting, for example, becomes a shape much more crucial to the whole than the splintered planet it defines. In the upper right-hand corner, forms are treated with arbitrary intensity and emphasis on movement with astonishingly successful results.

The Cubists themselves had quickly jettisoned the primacy of the cube, but here the master of Fauvism and languorous odalisques opens the style to all shapes. He fastens witty diagrams of motion, like the four banded circles in the upper central section, as securely into place as a Romanesque stone-carver stuck a statue on a column – and with the same self-confident gesture.

There is an apocryphal story that Matisse, returning from an exhibition, described to some friends what the newcomers were doing and in diagramming and explaining the entries of Picasso and Braque gave Cubism its name. In *The Moroccans* he also gave it a still-unmeasurable longevity.

No new program is presented in the picture, as there is in the works of the Futurists – an Italian manifesto-movement whose brief and violent life in the years preceding World War I produced a little greatness and a good deal of confusion. Their writings and paintings were full of ideas – to suggest the nobility and idealized force of a machine by superimposing its various lines

22 Henri Matisse
The Moroccans, 1916

Abstract painting

23 Pablo Picasso

Three Musicians, 1921

of action one beside the other; to bring the spectator "into the picture" so that he would see it in the same way as he sees fellow passengers sitting and standing all about him in a trolley-car. But such ideas of "ideas" seem to suggest an academic point of view, revealing a loss of tradition in the very act of attempting to be different. Matisse does not play with combinations or attitudes. The old campaigner, although a bit unfamiliar with the terrain, is still a general, and takes command accordingly.

Picasso's *Three Musicians* [fig. 23], 1921, is a much more famous, equally important, if not as successful picture. It, too, is prophetic, but of the directions away from Cubism, and foretells the return of literature to art. Resemblance to nature traditionally is achieved by a series of similes ("this tree is like that one"); here the operative images are metaphorical ("this arrangement is a storm at sea") and allow themselves the incon-

sistencies of allusion and invention that the conception of metaphor permits.

The setting is still Paris, but the time has changed. The sense of security within the avant-garde is as unshaken as ever; the belief in continuity is as deep and as familiar as in a well-regulated university. But the note of mocking optimism is somewhat harsher, as if, while his prestige was flourishing, the artist had begun to doubt the validity of the accepted positions of philistines vs. artists, and the eventual tributes.

At first Picasso's construction seems familiar in its modernity. The textured dog under the table which arises again at the left seems like a buttress exposed to indicate space flowing backward and still upward. Cut-out forms repeat colors or complement and reverse rhythms to start motions off across the large surface. But acrobatics soon stop; repetitions and variations appear to have little meaning in themselves; the dancing yellows abruptly appear artificial; forms disintegrate into verbal references. The whole composition, if observed from the station of Cubism, becomes chaotic or, worse, oversimplified and redundant (and this manner, appropriately, has been labelled Synthetic Cubism). What remains, after the fade-out of structure, are three strange and wonderful musicians and their dog and as soon as the masqueraders assume control, the image resumes functioning. The artist does not unmask his maskers, but disguises them as patiently and as cleverly as Velasquez might have done. The structure that is displayed is *not* the structure of the picture, but rather the fantastic anatomies of three elegant apparitions. Little plucking hands, stiff mediaeval vests and clever hats, even the dog's wagging tail, have arrived at the conventional secret unity of form and content. A diagram of the composition of M. Uhde's portrait would be a rather childish sketch of the finished work. But if one reduced *Three Musicians* to such a schoolroom exercise, one would arrive at a pattern of vertical and horizontal lines which meet supporting diagonals at various positions (where the metaphor becomes especially allusive) – and the whole chart would have little resemblance to the picture.

Cubism is like an ascending stair to a platform from where one may see in all directions. Matisse, in one instance, will face toward the gesture of creation, and find a completely integrated and intricate image within the reference of the painter's action. Picasso, in one of his phases, veils again the creative act with the secrecy of the master-craftsman's studio, and returns the ambiguity of literature to that of form.

The step that Cubism took away from Cézanne and from easily ascertainable resemblances of shape in paint to shape in nature was, in a sense, as liberating a one as that taken by the early Renaissance masters. In leaving the flat wall-surface of the Gothic artists, the fourteenth-century Florentines were free to make ample gestures within ever more complicated vistas of perspective, or to study the human body with the same delight and wonder that inspired the Carolingian miniaturists to investigate symbols of divinity. The Cubists, in making the picture independent of a specific environment, were able at the same time to take the act of painting itself, and the knowledge and inspiration that goes into this act, as their theme. Repetition of form or hue is as rewarding a device in the visual image as it is in a fugue, and in Picasso's *Still-life with Guitar* [fig. 24], 1913, the split-8 shape of the guitar's side appears five times in different angles, colors, weights, and positions in space. The act of building a guitar into the picture becomes so important that the guitar itself is only alluded to.

In this process of creative construction, the idea of space in painting became radically changed. Picasso shows how it can be made in depth, going into the wall or projected into the room, but during the very demonstration, the illusive element is contradicted almost as soon as it is established. Thus the sound-hole of the guitar in the center of the picture is drawn as if it were about an inch thick, and seen from the left – the lower right section of its thickness being prominently displayed. However, after we accept this, the represented thickness will seem to become a dark disc, flat above its dark background, on top of which a white circle has been placed – for the strings of the guitar cast a shadow on the white. Background has become foreground, and will, with only a little continued observation, be a middle-ground, and then jump from one to the other depending on the spectator's interpretation of all the contiguous elements. Yet though motion works continually backward and forward, the illusion is seldom carried beyond a few inches; nor

Abstract painting

is it allowed to establish a permanent hole or jut on the surface. Such emphasis on space is one of the most important characteristics of abstract painting, and here is true abstraction, for our visual perception of distance in nature has been entirely reorganized to the needs of the painter.

In *Still-life with Guitar,* however, not only does each form have its identifiable allusion to the everyday world, but certain forms are actually taken from parts of this world. Lettering, cut from posters and labels, is pasted on the picture to exist as itself, and as a pictorial unit in the scheme of the whole. It has been suggested that this was an act of proud derision on the part of Picasso and Braque (the latter had been trained as a professional letterer), but this hardly seems likely when one takes into account the seriousness with, and high level of accomplishment at which they were working. Rather such an introduction of absolute reality into the abstraction seems a logical step from the creation of a continually ambiguous scaffolding of space. In the Picasso, the fragmented letters resemble abstract elements; they also recall the appurtenances of the café still-life – the things seen and drunk at the marble-top table. Too, in this picture the large letters are surprinted over smaller type, so the pasted elements themselves can join in the play of background-foreground. But there is no "pure" form in *Still-life with Guitar;* the pasted papers are fragments of environment that any Parisian could pick up by the thousand. And Picasso carefully gives each piece a place to itself in the structure so that it can keep intact all references to its previous existence.

Braque's *Still-life with Newspaper* [fig. 25], 1912, goes even further. Two sections of newsprint, a piece of simulated-wood wallpaper, and a strip of dark paper are the main materials. The fold of the left-hand paper is modelled emphatically – an illusion immediately denied by the in-

tersection of the contour of a bottle, which adopts the modelling for its own unfinished edge. The lower left corner of the wallpaper also appears raised above its charcoal shadow. But Braque is willing to risk this inconsistency, for the quickest inspection of the picture's surface convinces that the wallpaper is pasted on the advertisement below it, and is intercepting no light from the upper right corner. The third piece of paper is cut into the familiar guitar contour, and one of the reasons Braque used dark paper here was surely to show at its best the jagged, hacked quality of the edge – not only do we know it is cut paper, but the artist must even suggest the act of cutting and reveal the slicing of the scissors.

Denying the concept of duty to reality in nature, Braque can use this reality itself – in abandoning the subject for the object, the object is made out of the subject.

As they evolved the most abstract art, as far as the motive is concerned, that history had known, the Cubists felt impelled to bring undisguised reality into the picture. By whirling a bottle, or a glass, or a table-top around and through invented planes, they also could increase the spectator's palpable sensation of the subject. But when they used the object in nature itself as a material, they could increase this contact to an immediacy which had been lost in art since the seventeenth century, and the emergence of the popular *belle matière.* It is interesting to observe that in the Braque collage, the most abstract and the least allusive shapes are described by the conventional means of charcoal on white paper, and these are exactly the elements that define the bottle, the glass, and the table. The sections of newsprint and wallpaper, on the other hand, are assigned less realist roles, and work more as shapes of uninterpretable space. This was, evidently, one of the artist's solutions to the problem of bringing totally associative elements into the picture: he

24 Pablo Picasso

Still-life with Guitar, 1913, collage

Abstract painting

25 Georges Braque

Still-life with Newspaper, 1912, collage

let only the abstract ones tell the brief, delicate story of Parisian life, 1912.

The associative form will, of course, cling to all associations, and it is expected to; it is, in fact, always amusing to read collages – and usually they are made with type helpfully right-side up. Braque's still-life informs us of the possibility of buying a sewing machine "American made . . . the only perfect one . . . universally famous . . . ten year guarantee . . . 20 centimes a day . . ." There is also an ad for curing *"les maladies de la femme"* and a hint concerning the necessity of looking for the proper label before buying *"Poudres de Cock."* In another collage, by Picasso, one part of the pasted-on newspaper tells of a pacifist demonstration by some Socialist students; further down the picture is an article on the progress of whatever Balkan War was then current. Here a more complicated irony was attempted – but in general such additional offerings of content seem

only lagniappes, to be read at one's leisure; rests from the serious business of looking at the picture.

Such works remind many spectators of nineteenth- and late eighteenth-century *trompe-l'œil* paintings, like the Bruff [fig. 13], or the more famous productions of Harnett, or some North Italian and Dutch still-lifes. Indeed, the Cubists frequently went out of their way to "fool the eye," and in Picasso's *Guitar and Glasses* [fig. 26], 1913, a fake printed headline is painted on the surface and a piece of fake wood-textured wallpaper is painted at the bottom of the canvas. Picasso, of course, is not concerned with the tight brushwork of the realists, and it is quickly evident that this oval picture is all paint on canvas. But a spectator, prepared for Picasso's collages, could be tricked into assuming that this was another one – an illusion that the artist has planned even more carefully in several other paintings. Bruff's means and ends have their own motives, which

26 Pablo Picasso

Guitar and Glasses, 1913

have nothing to do with resemblance to Picasso. The nineteenth-century artist lures us into a complicated visual game of tag, hoping always to catch the spectator shaking his head, with a hand tentatively raised to scratch the painted surface in disbelief that a real object is not pasted there. The world of the picture must play at being the world of the spectator, lulling him into a mood of effortless marvelling by staying commonplace. Picasso also uses commonplace objects as his starting point, but his painting will be anything but amusingly recognizable to his contemporaries.

Here, once more, glasses and a guitar are furiously possessed by the painter who turns them to every position, capturing intermediate shifts of angles, superimposing a top view on a side one, flooding the narrow oval space with an amazed, amazing community of stems, flutings, mouths and bases – all laced together momentarily by short ovals, only to resume, a second later, the

backward-forward play of form and allusion. Above this the letters "ARMAGNAC" and "JOUR [nal]" are spread like transparent overlays dissolved in pigment. They refer, again, to the café life – the newspaper and after-dinner brandy. But their function is also their very transparency, which adds another motif and another possibility to the complication of space. And here, as in the Braque collage, actuality is used as the most abstract element, while the least recognizable forms are those most closely connected with the evocation of glass, bottle, guitar, and table.

Since Braque and Picasso's initial introduction of the known into the unknown, the collage technique has played a long, distinguished role in modern art.

The recent book illustrations for *Jazz* by Matisse were made of cut-out, brightly colored paper; the material is used for its own sake – there are no illusions, no recollections, no pauses for reading

45

27 Henri Matisse

Icarus, 1946, collage

small print. But the sharp edges, and the insistence on the pasted joints in *Icarus* [fig. 27], 1946, recalls some Cubist innovations. And it is fitting that Matisse in his old age should take up this medium invented by once-shocking youth. In a way, *Icarus* seems to be sculpture of flat paper – and, after its suggestion, so do the early collages of Picasso and Braque.

George Grosz' image [fig. 28], is at the opposite extreme from Matisse's. It was executed in 1932 when the artist was still captivated by the fireworks of the German Dada group (the idea was up-with-art by down-with-other-art, no questions answered, and it acted like a new broom among the tired aesthetics of the Swiss and German patron classes. Ironically, this creative and energetic movement became respectable upon contact with the assured poise, charm, and appetite of Paris. Dada was, in the thirties, that great city's *dernièr cris,* under the more sonorous name of Surrealism – the label was Apollinaire's – and under the leadership of a twentieth-century Bossuet, André Breton). Here prints and photo-engravings, torn and sliced, pasted one next to the other, create a fabulous Hollywood dream-sequence. As in the Matisse, the material counts for everything, but with Grosz, everything is *except* the pictorial. The moon is a lipstick smile; the bound corpse, like Phlebas, travels the water; the lighthouse is an incongruous prison of hope; a lion's maw is a trivial cloud; flowers are in the flood. Literary associations, with the greatest ease of optical interpretation, are the basic units of this self-consciously demoniac poem. It would be wrong to say that the line between the verbal and the visual image has ceased to exist – for in *The Lighthouse of Bornholm and the Floating Boatsman* there are no pictorial elements. By insisting on the real life of each snippet of paper (just as Cézanne had insisted on the real life of each stroke of the brush), Grosz produces a stage set

28 George Grosz

*The Lighthouse of Bornholm and the
Floating Boatsman, 1932, collage*

for drama. The collage is freed from the painter, who abandons painting to become a director in new medium, most related to the theater and the motion picture.

The late Matisse and the Dada Grosz stand at extremes; it remained for the highly poetic and sensitized eye of Kurt Schwitters to find a middle ground. Also starting in the Dada group, Schwitters saw a good deal more than ironic jokes in the rediscovery of the commonplace. It was all very well for such brilliant innovators as Marcel Duchamp or Max Ernst to set lessons for aging Cubists, Post-Impressionists, stockbrokers, or couturiers, and demonstrate that the only true quality of art is heroic imagination. "Look again at Lautréamont," urged the Surrealists. "When he wanted to describe the beauty of freshly encountered youth, he did not appeal to some myth, planet, or vegetable; he evoked the fortuitous encounter of a sewing machine and an umbrella on an operating table."

The "fortuitous" and the "commonplace" . . . the latter had existed in collages since the beginning, the former, perhaps, also, for the Surrealists only underlined and, paradoxically, attempted a disciplined exploitation of the automatic elements in the creative act.

For Schwitters, the fortuitous was an easily forgotten characterization. It may be as hard to recognize a well-done act as it is to do it. At any rate, his plan was based on his materials, and he sought the commonplace with the spotter's eye and the passion of a great butterfly collector. Bits of paper – old transfer tickets, postmarks, pieces of newsprint, handbills, stationery, posters – every sort of trash and litter, colored by ink, rain, mud, and sun, were carefully scrutinized, categorized, and, if accepted, picked up and stored in boxes which became palettes for collages. The action, although highly refined, is almost universal, and almost everyone has been intrigued by some eye-

Abstract painting

29 Kurt Schwitters

Merz, 33, 1920, collage

catching piece of flattened, torn envelope or sign, lying in a gutter or pasted on a wall. Of course Schwitters' process of selection was a good deal easier, for he simply appropriated supplies; most of us are only attracted by the finished product – the collage *trouvé*, which is anything but commonplace.

The artist's disposition of materials on his surface was made with an uncanny exactness of measurement, both for the literary, or associative weight of the object itself, and for its weight as a material, colored and formed, in a relationship with other colors and shapes. If one plotted *Merz, 33** [fig. 29], 1920, as a graph, one would find that the crucially verbal elements rest on the strongest points of the structure, and also that their directional pushes and pulls (as the type reads, or as the heart points) have been reconciled with the more purely pictorial dynamics.

Schwitters found he could have his cake and eat it; his only punishment was that it would not be a very large portion. The medium is limited by the simple "either/or" potential of the materials – either a postage cancellation on an envelope or a black triangle. At his best, Schwitters could keep the allusions dancing between the possibilities, and, perhaps, even a third, as a shape would suggest another material, or echo some familiar gesture. But the heavy restrictions are there – as they must be on an art that will be wholly interpretive, both verbally and pictorially – and Schwitters, like Paul Klee, was perfectly content to operate within these boundaries. The most obvious limit is that of scale. A Carolingian miniaturist could make a two-inch figure two miles high, but here a torn transfer ticket is a torn transfer ticket, especially as Schwitters delights in every nuance and detail of its history.

*
Like many abstractionists, Schwitters relied on a system of identification by numbers instead of titles, keeping *Merz,* a Dada nonsense syllable, as a general title and trademark.

30 Piet Mondrian

Composition in Line, 1913

One could imagine Léger using such subject-matter for a vast post-office mural, but the Frenchman would so generalize, so abstract the elements of the collage palette that Schwitters could only consider it an act of blasphemy. His material must *be* real. Some of the other restrictions are those of allusion and illusion. Picasso or Rembrandt or Titian "cheat" to their hearts' content: they can baffle us, disguise their means, shift our attention from the hand that stuffs a rabbit into the top-hat, discourse on an infinity of topics, avoid forever a point of total understanding – and this is due to the flexibility of their medium, rather than to their genius, although their genius surely demanded just this flexibility. Schwitters' frame of reference is really a frame, binding the creator within it. Naturally, the spectator may range at will, and Schwitters' collages can become starting points for long interpretations. But then the interpreter in Schwitters and in the spectator be-

come artists, and the collages, when all is finished, might seem even more restricted. Still, it is ungrateful to insist upon narrowness when the height reached is so great. The artist was not only able to discover and exploit a new reality in the terms of a lost reality, and to extend the range of the modern artist's opportunities, but he stood at a crossroad and, almost unnoticed, found a fifth passage to satisfaction.

Collage took from Cubism a method and an attitude towards the picture and its materials that were and still are used in a number of manners to create abstractions out of undisguised reality. The next five pictures illustrated here [figs. 30 to 34] also start from Cubism, but go from it to a way of painting (often it was also a rigorous, almost monastic way of life) that would systematically expel all resemblances to objects in nature from the image.

Abstract painting

31 Kasimir Malevich

*Suprematist Composition, Two Squares,
1913, drawing*

The Cubist attitude toward the subject is invariably ambivalent. Natural colors and values, for example, were abandoned in the early stages for a restricted palette of tans and greys. But within such self-imposed limitations, modelling, outlining with black, and meticulously plotted highlights of pure ocher or swashes of dimmed purple continually referred to those heightened sensations that historically have been accepted as the artists' birthday present of insight into everyday life. The Cubists' conception of space was abstract, and their activation of the surface into forward, backward, and lateral motions was more a revelation of the picture's dynamics than those of a still-life or a human face. Still, at some point, Picasso's pipe or the guitar can be picked up, or the carafe contain wine.

Mondrian, the noble believer in order, progress, and, above all, equilibrium, rejected any such acceptance or exploitation of ambiguity. Working away from Cubism, he found a straight road which he always believed would lead eventually to the mountain-top from where a new sunrise of civilization could be greeted. To him the mystery was a perfection of vital (as against inert) balance, and he was willing to make any sacrifices for its celebration. *Composition in Line* [fig. 30] was painted in 1913, three years after the artist had made his first contact with Cubism in Paris. Like a Picasso or a Braque, it started with a conventional subject – here the façade of a cathedral. Unlike the Cubists', however, Mondrian's every change is a remove from the façade in order to assert the supremacy of the picture's action. The simplest ideas of naturalist space are denied by such methods as refusing the image any definition at the edges of the canvas, so that the whole structure floats on the surface, like straws on water; or by reversing conventional foreshortening, making the more distant parts of the façade at the top of the painting smaller and

32 **Theo van Doesburg**

*Design for a Stained-Glass Window,
1924, watercolor*

clearer than those at the foreground bottom; in fact, when seen upside-down, the composition takes on so increased a resemblance to architecture that one might easily suspect one of the artist's ways of avoiding entanglements with the motif was by reversing it in just this way. Except for a very few arcs, which seem to cushion the slow, bounding rhythms up and down the painting, lines are vertical or horizontal and angles are all 90 degrees. Mat pigment is applied almost independently of the linear framework, spreading behind or over it in its own play of released and restrained attention, and color and form fuse only after a long process of adjustment and correction. *Composition in Line* bears all the evidence of this labor – for Mondrian was still Cubist enough to delight in it. Some edges almost fade away under the awkward, feathery application of paint, flicks of the brush bring one rectangle to the same life as its neighbors, others are subdued – almost wiped away – as the painter's eye, searching for the image's equilibrium, constantly adjusts each element towards the final unity.

The cathedral façade is still present, and sunlit stones inform the play of whites across *Composition*. But this is only background material, like Purchas' *Pilgrimage* is background to "Kubla Khan." It is just a step to forget the cathedral altogether, and start inventing from the start.

Such a renunciation of nature for pure invention has fascinated many philosophers who see it as an act of self-destruction, or engagement to art, or to morality, or what-not. Actually this break (first made in 1910, by Kandinsky, it is believed) was more like a friendly divorce. If Mondrian's cathedral was nothing but a point of departure, and if it entailed considerable planning to keep the building from obtruding where it was not wanted, why not do away with it?

Contrariwise, why do away with it . . .?

Only a year after his exposure to Cubism, the

Abstract painting

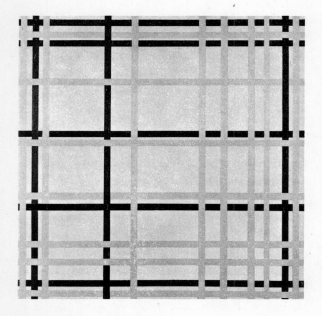

33 Piet Mondrian

New York, 1942

Russian Kasimir Malevich made the drawing *Two Squares* [fig. 31], 1913. Superficially, it would seem that this is a logical reduction, but to absurdity. Surely the picture is complete in itself, but what is left of it; what remains of all the colors and secrets and body of knowledge that had been handed down since the Renaissance, and that had been even further enriched by all those civilizations of early history the painters themselves had discovered? Only pencil on paper, only two squares, a rectangle, some slight variations of texture indicated by the graphite rubbed and scraped over the white pores, the paper itself, the descriptive title, and a general one, *Suprematist Composition*. One can understand why connoisseurs, confronted with this drawing, would mourn for the lost, denied, beautiful image of a beautiful man. The artist seems to repulse every attempt by the spectator to live his own life in front of the picture; he must take art, or leave it, for exactly what it is.

Yet *Suprematist Composition, Two Squares* is not quite so simple – not even for its creator. "I have invented nothing," wrote Malevich. "I only felt night within me, and in it I perceived that new thing which I have named 'Suprematism.' This was expressed by a black surface that represented a square."

"Night within me" sounds more like the hero of *The Possessed* than the behaviorist with his salivating dogs, and Malevitch, from the perspective of four decades, seems more akin to Dostoevski than to Pavlov. The step – like Alice's across a brook in Looking Glass country – may have been a short and easy one, but it brought a sensation of miraculous novelty as well as a sense of the greatness of the present, and of the future. The artist was especially aware of the negative mystique in his squares – they are not ikons, they are not picnics on the grass, they are not clever decorations for the taste of the moment, nor passive pieces of middle-class furniture. They are two honest squares, pencil on paper, executed with expert craftsmanship (although it is not extremely difficult to become expert at this particular craft) in a preconceived fashion. "What else," Malevich could ask, "are the Arena frescoes?" And his question cannot be answered as quickly as one might think.

Not through logic and not through some vulgar laws of harmonious decoration, without swooning to a Bach fugue or reading Blavatsky, Malevich found the darkness in his soul was black squares. Art, he felt, liberated from convention and led by genius, would be a universal language with its own vocabulary of color, shape, pattern, etc. With this language any emotion could be expressed, and anyone could read it who was not too blinded by prejudice: thus the strong bonds between non-objective painting and radical political movements.

The results were according to our notions of each man's talents – notions that may change with time (Malevich, for example, today appears to be a rather dull painter). But that the step away from nature was a brief, exhilarating act was enthusiastically demonstrated almost as soon as Cubism had found the opening.

The social aspects of non-objective (i.e. without recognizable subject matter) painting are of considerable importance. It is ironic that while the public may have pined for long-vanished fare of expert visualizations, the one movement that supplied them was Surrealism, a school openly contemptuous of the public (although the Surrealists officially espoused Communism, for they could only conceive of the public as the bourgeois elite, which they hoped Communism would explode). The only style that claimed to offer a means of direct communication with the masses – the non-objective one – popularly has been considered the most hermetic and snobbish of all. The average

man loves Dali – who despises him – and if the average man were forced to attend a van Doesburg exhibition he would hate it – yet this artist did everything possible to make his work a functioning part of society.

Architect, poet, critic, and typographer as well as painter, Theo van Doesburg was one of the most creative geniuses of this century. But so many-sided and inexhaustible (except for time, for he died in 1931, aged forty-seven) were his talents that to summarize his contribution would require a much-needed book. His *Design for a Stained-Glass Window* [fig. 32], 1924, can represent the lengths to which non-objective artists went in order to "pass the word"; to reveal the new-found freedom and integration of artist in society that had been discovered just a step away from Cubism.

The design is Gothic in its suggestion of soaring height, and also in its articulation of structural components and psychological function. Blocks of color, in what seem to be relatively simple repeats, but which are really fantastically complicated and imaginative variations (try to find two identical rectangles), create a drama of light which surpasses a great deal of the much-praised mediaeval window decorations. But here the point is not so much one of practical success – for most of van Doesburg's projects were never executed – but of motive. The non-objective artist eagerly invaded every aspect of life and – as has been so often explained in museum exhibitions – succeeded in revolutionizing our environment in an amazingly short time. Skyscrapers, linoleum, magazine layouts, lamps, even the mirrors in restaurant rest-rooms (whose designs are perhaps the most sensitive barometers of a style's acceptance), all take their various streamlined angles because such men as van Doesburg insisted that art must act on every thing. And once the non-objectivists succeeded, every other style followed

Abstract painting

34 Ben Nicholson

Still-life (Punch and Judy Show), *1932-37*

– either impressing its forms on fashion or being pirated for them by fashion's impresarios. Yet *Design for a Stained-Glass Window,* by its very intensity and compelling originality, transcends its place in fashion and its social use. This modern artist played a heroic role that had been forgotten since the time of Rubens. Refusing the parts of Hamlet or Coriolanus, he reiterated the classical lines of the man of action in the good state. There is no priggishness in this attitude, and van Doesburg did not indulge in escapist gibes at better talents in Ivory Towers (the final thrust of the mediocre artist) ; he was a member of the Dada group with Schwitters as well as a planner of model houses, but he found full expression, with all the mysteries and mockeries inherent in such achievement, in a completely social attitude.

In achievement there is also release, and it is not surprising that van Doesburg's fusion of the aesthetic act with the social one should result in countless followers taking up a thread here and a clue there – being accepted by the public for an easy translation, or by aficionados for a clever transposition. Still van Doesburg's position, his example as well as production, is crucial for our time.

It remained for Mondrian – a far greater painter than Malevich, a far longer life than van Doesburg's – firmly to establish a totally non-figurative, geometric style in the realms of modern painting. Continuing to evolve the motifs stated in such early works as *Composition in Line,* he dedicated himself to combinations of straight, ribbonlike areas of color – usually of pure hue – or of black on white backgrounds, all intersecting at 90 degrees. The resulting pictures, such as *New York* [fig. 33], 1942, arrived at their definition after long periods of exacting work. Stacks of unfinished canvases left in Mondrian's

35 Pablo Picasso

The Red Tablecloth, 1924

studio after his death (in New York in 1944) reveal what a hesitant, even painful process of self-criticism his method entailed. Working with charcoal on canvas, and later with tape, each bar was permitted to rest in place only after being shifted in and out, across, up and down, as if the artist felt he must actually visualize and destroy all but one combination before deciding he was satisfied. Behind the most minor assignments of space in a Mondrian there seems to exist a gigantic parade of approximations – many of them as convincing as the ultimate choice – which inform the final image, just as the thousands of Rembrandt sketches inform each of that earlier Dutch master's paintings. This reticently delicate perception of interval was expressed by an equally sensitive technique. The surface of Mondrian's paint – at times clumsy and haphazard, at times astonishingly sophisticated – is always knowingly varied, for despite the avowed impersonality of

his aims, the artist never impinged upon his realization of the Mondrian personality – a great European painter.

Lines cross the white background and each other at the central areas of the picture, going outward to the edges – often they are painted on to the stretcher right around the corner of the canvas – and then proceed, never meeting again, into imagined space. It is only on the picture – and here may be a symbolic action of Mondrian's images in equilibrium – that they meet, as if these very surfaces were magnetic fields of reality through which pass idealized infinities of parallel lines. And the individual field must be exquisitely adjusted, for the artist invariably denies the absolute point of balance toward which most contemporary realist painters strive. It is as easy to find the top of a Mondrian as any careful landscape; his pictures appear completely out of kilter upside-down or on their sides. Even

Abstract painting

36 Wassily Kandinsky

Black Lines, 1913

set upright, the ending of play and counterplay in rest is avoided – perhaps to increase the outward velocity of the ribbons of color. It has been said that Mondrian empties himself and his spectators by too complete a statement – there is nothing left; no further questions; class dismissed. I find that in his very cultivation of uncertainty, and in his consistent refusal to put in place the last weight that stops the scales from oscillating, he was able to keep the strictest, coldest masterpieces human, and thus finally impenetrable.

After Kandinsky, Mondrian, van Doesburg and so many others, non-objective painting became a true international style, practiced both beautifully and stupidly in almost every part of the world. Ben Nicholson, for example, one of England's most distinguished painters, has found ample scope to display his cultured sense of edge and tone within its so-called confines. *Still-life (Punch and Judy Show)* [fig. 34], 1932-37 (although half a bowl and perhaps a table obtrude on this usually non-figurative stage) , reveals what a personal stamp an artist can affix on the basic requirements of the idiom. Razor-sharp lines between smoky colors, the exactly tilted rectangle which is corrected (one can almost hear the precise "click") by the darker background form, a calculated use of empty space as a showcase effect – all bear the hallmark of Nicholson. In America, Albers (after a long teaching career in Germany, which he is now continuing at Yale) , Glarner (who follows those investigations of the slant he started in Paris almost thirty years ago), Burgoyne Diller, George Cavallon, Harry Holtzman, Jean Xceron, and many others are continuing to prove the vitality and originality possible in this direction – which is so often proclaimed the dead end of modern art. And such non-objective painting still exerts a commanding influence on contemporary design – from ashtrays to tombs. One of the ironies of modern art will be the

37 Jean Arp

Arpaden, 1918-22

refusal of a child in 1982 to see anything in a Mondrian but the façade of a famous building.

The concept of the collage and the non-objective point of view were not the only movements to emerge from Cubism, for Cubism continues, and, as Alfred H. Barr, Jr. has pointed out, places the amoeba next to the cube. Even while Picasso was working at some of his most severely analytical paintings, in which each piece seems to have been notched and fitted into the slanting schemes of facets, with every angle neatly articulated, he painted a few pictures where points relaxed into curves and where the pulling tensions of construction were reversed into the more relaxed ones of swollen, outward-pushing ovoids. Then, as the enthusiastic disciplines of Cubism were relaxed, forgotten, and recalled again for new purposes, the cube was banished almost as completely as the curve had been a decade before. In *The Red Tablecloth* [fig. 35], 1924, the manipulation of perspective, texture and pigment are expected extensions of Cubism, but except for the indication of the depth of the table at the bottom of the canvas, and the by-then conventional use of interpenetrating planes and colors, the picture presents an entirely different sense of, and attitude toward form. Undulating, repeating ovals with suggestions of floating informality, amoeba-like reachings of objects into space (like the melon out of the window) or into each other (note how the guitar's curve is frankly echoed in the wallpaper above), all seem to be reactions from Cubism rather than foreseeable developments of its premises. The picture no longer insists on its independence as an object in bounded space, now it insists on being able to do anything it wants to, whenever it so desires. It will be frivolous or highly dramatic, it will tease the eye with certain especially attractive passages, or peremptorily withdraw from large areas which are merely sustaining intervals between climaxes.

The first World War is over, the century is finally well on its way. Paris is the scene of brilliant exhibitions, ballets, cocktail parties, concerts, scandals, theaters, cafés. A tough, old generation, with Degas and Renoir finally dead (in 1917 and 1918 respectively; although Monet lived to 1926) is gone; a new generation is already coughing and stamping in the wings, and it seems to be as perversely brilliant as ever. Evil becomes a topic for debating teams, not armies, and leisure is a reality. The artist willingly accepts his historical privilege to find beauty in any direction his inspiration moves, and he urges his inspiration to investigate freely. A monument to middle-class pleasure can be as superb as the sparse, metaphysical severities of the avant-garde, and Picasso proves it.

In Kandinsky's *Black Lines* [fig. 36], 1913, the other force behind the movement that has been called "free-form abstraction" makes its appearance. This Russian-born scientist and mystic was allied with the German Expressionist group (which is discussed later in this section) and had been much influenced by Monet.

In 1906, he was in Paris and presumably observed the strenuous breaking with nature which was then about to come to a climax. However, where the French would posit a rationale, Kandinsky decided to trust a disciplined intuition. If he leaves the landscape – for these "black lines" are quite obviously derived from hills, trees, and clouds – it will be for the sensation in front of it and the painting, simultaneously. The image, from its first acceptance of drawing or color, will require or suggest other lines and colors, and the landscape, too, will present various exigencies and invitations. So the painter, in Kandinsky's case, chooses to be a sensitized medium between the material of paint and the emotion of sensation.

"Yet by what right," a logician may ask, "can the artist suspend his social responsibility of planning, ordering, and dominating?"

A familiar objection, once again, must be considered more relevant verbally than practically. It is impossible to predict and to organize a sustained creative action in which the entire mind and body of the creator are engaged. Even the most carefully rehearsed of paintings are surprisingly different from their preliminary aspects. "If you accept the possibility of an artist," Kandinsky might say, "then you must accept his production." A painter will sketch directly in front of nature, hurriedly, as Constable did, giving the trained hand complete liberty in order to capture a fleeting vision. Kandinsky's trained hand and eye tackled a subject less familiar to his contemporaries – a new object, the painting.

Furthermore, Kandinsky might add, his act of painting can be seen in a "purer" form, unadulterated by the irrelevancies of reproductive, copying gestures. Is not Titian's brushstroke that curls miraculously across some sky more eloquent than the one that imperceptibly defines the outline of a nose? But this is to be outrageously verbal at the other extreme, for the outline of the nose or the careful planning that surely did go into Kandinsky's *Black Lines* are of equal, if different importance.

Picasso's forms in *The Red Tablecloth* are free of the restraining cube, Kandinsky's, in *Black Lines* could be called free of the restraining plot. In both pictures the curve is dominant, and it ranges over the surface with buoyant, grasping energy. From these two sources comes a whole school of abstract art which is the reverse and the complement of Mondrian's and van Doesburg's abstractions.

In Jean Arp's insolent, witty, and ingratiating drawing, *Arpaden* [fig. 37], 1922, we meet again the spirit of Dada, but here in a cooler, more meditative mood. By contrast "the art of the

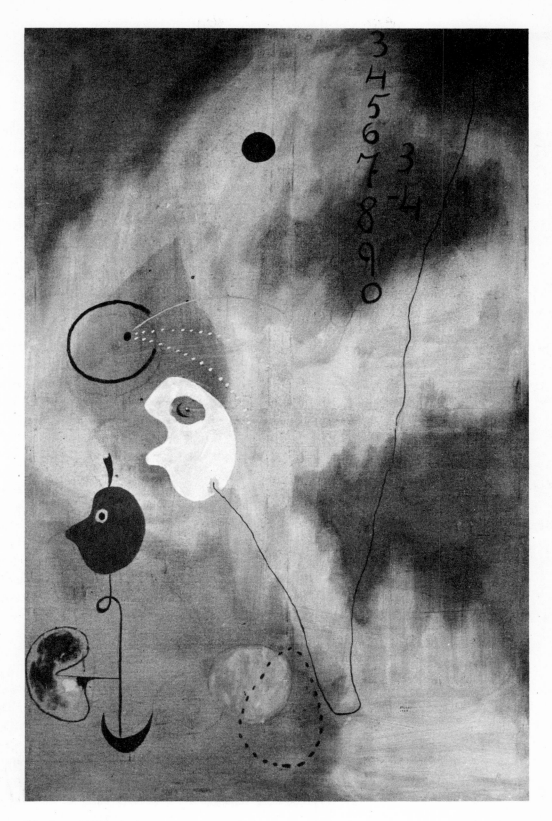

38 Joan Miró

Untitled painting, 1925

59

39 Pablo Picasso

Project for a Monument, 1928, drawing

bourgeois" is considered a "sanctioned lunacy." "Especially," Arp continues, from his position in the Dada group, "these naked men, women, and children in stone or bronze, exhibited in public squares, gardens, and forest clearings, who untiringly dance, chase butterflies, shoot arrows, hold out apples, blow the flute, are the perfect expression of a mad world." His program, which was called "Concrete Art," was "not to copy nature." "We do not want," Arp wrote, "to reproduce, we want to produce like a plant that produces a fruit . . . we want to produce directly and not through interpretation." Works of art "should not be signed by their creators." "These paintings, these sculptures, these objects, should remain anonymous in the great studio of nature like clouds, mountains, seas, animals, men.*"

It is difficult, however, for an artist to remain anonymous, or want to stay so, as Mondrian discovered, and Arp, the Alsatian sculpture, painter, and poet, does not have to sign his drawings; their eccentric, bulging curves and flipping extremities are so easily recognizable that today it is standard practice to identify "Arp-forms" in much contemporary architectural and furniture design. The imprint of the artist is so strong that even when he goes to the extremes of auto-creation (for example, dropping squares of paper on a surface and pasting the result together) his personality still can be easily perceived (for, to revert to the example, no one but Arp would have accepted just that arrangement for pasting).

Arpaden, however, does present a form that seeks independence in nature. The first strategy in this separation is wit, for seriousness – on the part of the spectator – inevitably summons the whole effort of grappling with serious, boring work. In wit there are opportunities for tempo-

*

From *On My Way* by Jean Arp, 1948, translated by Ralph Manheim.

rary withdrawals by the artist in front of his picture. He can dress-up an effect that momently will shock or amuse – for shock and amusement, in painting, as in such other visual presentations as the theatre and the dance, are justifiable, if not essential elements of the aesthetic emotion. Like Falstaff, the artist can play several parts at once, and the widest range of invention is open to his genius for elaboration and irony. The danger is in arousing the fury of the Puritans, who insist on the importance of appearing earnest. Arp, like so many sculptors, painters, and poets of today, successfully avoided this risk by completely accepting the social role assigned the dedicated artist – and the Puritans, sooner or later, are bound to respect anyone who has been willing to live uncomfortably.

In the curve, Arp found a way to express completed action, to be as frivolous as a Rococo master (the name of whose style comes from the freely curving seashell, *rocaille* – a favorite Arp subject) and still retain the possibilities of a monumental style. The Cubists would exalt the "hows" of creating; Arp also exposes the happy accidents; in fact he assiduously hunts for them. But his selection of results is unique, personal, and affirmative. *Arpaden* is a symptom, not a measure of the artist's capabilities. Almost a personification of free-form abstraction, it also must epitomize the limits of Arp's vision, which are those inherent in an extraordinarily refined taste.

It remained for such a painter as Miró to fuse the swelling curve, the plays on chance, the nose-thumbing, and the desperately engaged expression into a major style. In the untitled canvas of 1925 [fig. 38], taut, shivering lines, columns of numerals, two heads that rise like balloons in amazement, and an eye that shoots out dots, all float on the painted surface in bundles of form. The composition is deceptively simple. Objects, fixed on the flattened, loosely brushed back-ground – they appear to float about three inches above it – are ordered in space by what can be likened to gravitational force. Large and small shapes hold each other in position by the pulls, from all sides, of the other elements; and inner tensions thus activated also become elastic arcs of motion. The wit of this Catalonian, who was a semi-member of the Surrealist group in Paris, but whose independence of thought always excluded him from the inner-chambers of the movement, is a liberating technical factor, as it is in Arp. He can meticulously adjust the most difficult tones and lines, work with the apprehension of a Swiss watch-maker, but still, in the elegant gesture of laughing it off, successfully avoid pedantry and academicism – traces of which are sometimes noticeable in his pictures. It is not that Miró minimizes the importance of effort; he refuses to inflate it, and, in the process, elevates the responses of humor and fantasy to the level of important expression, from which they practically had been excluded since the beginning of the nineteenth century.

Yet Miró's accomplishment has been much more than the acceptance of an attitude. Because he is one of the greatest craftsmen of the century, he was able to bring all species of soft forms into his painting. The most trivial, infantile forehead-nose-chin silhouette can be endowed with the grandeur of an Attic divinity, and he can make some intricate composition, which would delight all erudite non-objectivists, seem effortless and insouciant.

When so great a talent works in a comparatively restricted range of shape and scheme (there are no restrictions on Miró's accomplishments in cultivating his garden), it is to be expected that a highly influential style will result. The amoebic cusps and dents, the prodigious technical invention, the Christmas-colors, the changes, which snap like a whip, from tight to loose application

Abstract painting

40 Alexander Calder

A New Alphabet of Forms, 1942, drawing

of paint, the suggestions of contained, but swelling strength within a constellation of forms, all these, and many other Miró-marks, are characteristic of the final phase of abstract art in the International School of Paris between-two-wars.

Miró took the free-form, which Picasso was probably the first to introduce, and made it the keystone of a style. Later Picasso, the older Spaniard, would use it to smash a style. In the paintings and drawings of his so-called "Bone Period," like *Project for a Monument* [fig. 39], dated August 2, 1928, the artist returns to illusionistic space, and with a vengeance. Revenge, perhaps against the too-long tradition of "painterliness," which was so apt to yield nothing but pretension; or against the younger Surrealist generation, showing them that the master was still younger than they when it came to paradox and invention; or by the ebullient bon-vivant within him against the wild-eyed, nervous-fin-

gered artist. Perhaps there was no revenge at all (for today one is apt to overemphasize Picasso's Spanishness), but simply another possibility exploited. But, at any rate, the units of free-form were suddenly blown up miles high, fitted into carnival floats of extremely funny anatomies, and presented to the world in a flood of pen drawings and tinted paintings. The method is academic illustration – extremely able, informed, and brilliantly eclectic.

The content, as in many Mirós, is mock-heroic – high pitched and affably overzealous, like an anthem played on flageolets and kettledrums. The results, as is usually the case with this protean artist, are sometimes banal, sometimes magnificent; and they were spread throughout the world, in a matter of months, in impressive magazines edited by distinguished poets.

The American sculptor Alexander Calder, whose "mobiles" are among the most engaging objets-d'art ever devised, translated the curves of Arp and Miró into metal, suspended them on wires – calling upon the same pleasurable know-how with which Americans design the most beautiful airplanes – and rightly became the rage of Paris. He, too, adapted the free-form style to a system of means, simplifying and clarifying the bended contours until they became tricks as useful and as learnable as linear perspective. His watercolor, *A New Alphabet of Forms* [fig. 40], 1942, is probably one of the best examples of this process of patenting and diffusion. Compare the letters of Calder's alphabet with *Arpaden* [fig. 37], which could also be considered a piece of a larger system, or with the Miró. There is an almost sleepy quality about the Calder; a restful, reticent pleasingness. When activity is urged, as in the vaguely triangular shape that grows out of the base, it is done by illustrative means – as in the Picasso [fig. 39], but with none of the grandiose pleasure in paradox that is so great a part of the Spanish Parisian's contribution.

We have arrived at the appetizing, commendable, trivial abstraction – the set-exercise for classrooms, the improvisation on a completely explored theme. And we are also, in chronology, in Paris occupied by the German army.

Picasso goes on painting in Paris, becomes a great figure of resistance, and even, it has been asserted, somewhat sabotages the enemy's war effort by using up bronze to cast his sculptures. Matisse hibernates in the south of France. The rumor is that Vlaminck, Segonzac, and Derain come off rather badly. Drieu la Rochelle proclaims the defeat with intellectual brilliance, and the others, Montherlant, Giono, and Céline on one side, Malraux, Paulhan, and Eluard on the other, are variously stained and cleaned, abject and heroic, until finally Paris, as a world symbol, is "engaged" in compromise, in the most existentialist sense of the verb. For the second time in

only twenty-five years, France's youth is killed or paralyzed or extremely apt to be either. Calder, the American; Miró, the Spaniard (both had returned to their native countries to work) ; Masson; Tanguy (both of whom came to America) ; Arp; and all the other middle-aged revolutionaries hold on to youth for the five years of war. With liberation or return from exile, and peace, Picasso, Matisse, Léger, Bonnard, and Braque, men in their sixties, seventies, and eighties, are welcomed back to their leadership, long accepted by the organizers of public taste (Picasso has appeared on the cover of *Time* magazine). The middle-aged generation assumes the anomalous position of arrived 'comers. For the younger generation, there is doubt.

Postwar Paris is no longer positive of a continuity of genius, either locally bred or attracted from abroad. Painters will always go to the Left Bank and the Louvre, but there is a difference when they come to examine and to learn, not to be born. Brilliant younger French artists are still at work, such as Balthus, and there have been notable appearances of postwar talents – Dubuffet, Lanskoy, De Staël, Tal Coat. But somehow, during the war years, either the grandparent generation devoured its descendants or destroyed their faith in continuity (for, fulfilling the warning of Apollinaire, most French painters now carry the corpse of Picasso or Matisse, or both, on their backs) , or the compromised blankness of the period produced a following attitude of pessimism. Today, some painters will tell you that the Parisian art-dealer system is so rotten that no self-respecting young genius would touch it. (The French gallery buys its artists' production at a bargain price, thus insuring their three meals a day. In America, dealers usually sell the artists' work on consignment, retaining one third of the price if sold from the gallery, and one quarter if sold by an artist from his studio. By buying

Abstract painting

41 Vincent van Gogh

Landscape in the Rain, 1889

the artists' work outright, often without commitment to show it, the French dealer does take a major role in forming the painters' reputation, which he is apt to misinterpret. Thus the seeming break in continuity is simply a refusal to exhibit.) Another painter will insist that his colleagues are so saturated with School of Paris grandeur that they exist on switches and combinations only – Picasso forms with Bonnard color, or Matisse composition with Picasso subjects, or Braque textures with Matisse color plus a soupçon of Picasso's raillery, etc. But excuses are made. Although no attacks were coming on – merely queries in good faith – the response is defensive: "We have not because . . ." or "We have, but still you must remember . . ."

Paris' hegemony, vital and beneficial as it was, and mourned as it must be, seems shattered. The whole idea of certainty, the confidence in being able to turn the trick at the last moment, or

being able to see the glorious reward in the work, or, at the very least, knowing that the winners were in the vicinity – have vanished. Paris 1950 becomes Rome 1800: a place one has to visit, where an artist can live. There the public respects his profession; patrons almost ferociously hunt for talents which can be encouraged. But once doubt enters, the whole climate changes; and doubt hangs liks a solid overcast over the sunny capital of France.

Two movements in modern painting, neither of which is particularly concerned with abstraction, and a local *mise-en-scene,* must still be fitted into our background.

The dilemma of the modern artist has been individual as well as social. In the Renaissance, the problem for a Perugino (who, it is believed, was an atheist) was to reconcile the demands of the patron – who was the main public – with the invitations of art. The blend he found had to be a compromise, but perhaps this compromise had a certain piquancy that would have been lacking had Perugino been able to explore the possibilities of *trompe-l'œil* and perspective to his heart's content. He was able to thrive on religious subject-matter by handing responsibility for it to his rulers, and to become Peruginoesque within it. As the patron became bored or confused by the contemporary artist – a quite rapid tendency that is popularly considered to have begun around 1789 – the artist lost his place in high society. The ascendant middle class wanted a vulgar glory that painters were reluctant to supply – usually because the middle class did not understand the proper way to go about being vulgarly glorious. That the great genius of Courbet should not have been able to do for the merchant-monarchs of Paris what Titian and Giorgione did for the doges of Venice is one of the surprises of modern painting. But the cagey Parisian bourgeois was always decades behind the times, or expressing his own genius in fantastic conglomerations of visual bric-a-brac, which only anonymous craftsmen were ambitious enough to undertake. Still, as in the classic family of *Buddenbrooks,* it takes only a generation to get a patron, and the great financier's grandson is apt to resemble Shelley.

The artist on his own is still an artist, he materializes his sensations and needs with bewildering energy and speed. Much has been made of the dizziness of the pace from David to Picasso, about a hundred and ten years, but the same time span leads from Masaccio to Michelangelo. The modern development seems faster because the Renaissance patrons kept pace, while today it is mainly the comparatively small bands of Buddenbrooks grandchildren who are interested.

Officially cold-shouldered by church and state, painters continued to perfect and enlarge a vocabulary for the easel-picture as an ultimate work of art – which in all probability they would have done while ensconced in the most integrated of societies, but perhaps somewhat more didactically. The language became eloquent, filled with possibilities. Watteau, Poussin, Velasquez, Rubens, Titian, Rembrandt – all the great past – became a subterranean river, bringing encouragement to each experiment. Finally someone spoke the phrase "Art for Art's Sake," and there was Whistler's shower of sparks, or his carefully detailed, rather pedestrian portraits with such ostentatious titles as *Study in Mauve.*

Here was and is the dilemma of the individual. He has his great new vocabulary, but still wants to say something in his native tongue. This ambivalence was brought to a spectacular and explosive solution by Vincent van Gogh, whose *Landscape in the Rain* [fig. 41], 1889, painted from a melancholy little cell in the asylum at St. Rémy, begins the series of Expressionist pictures illustrated here. Van Gogh starts in the freezing, regulated fields and stars of the North. He moves to Paris, where he looses all image in the gently dissolving methods of Impressionism, his period's *avant-garde,* and this evangelical Hollander was obsessed in his search for a bohemia of truth. Then he moves south to the sun and the crisis of image lost in manner. He would dedicate himself to nature and man, he would help the underprivileged, not only by becoming underprivileged, but by making visual tracts which could drain away doubts and anxieties, just as the story of the Last Judgment, carved on a Gothic tympanum, reassured the praying mother of Villon. But what of the vocabulary, the painting?

Van Gogh solved the problem by identifying his creative act with the image (much as Picasso would do in his early Cubist pictures, except that the image was crucial for van Gogh). The brush-

Abstract painting

42 Paul Gauguin

The Sacred Mountain, 1882

strokes of Monet fill *Landscape in the Rain,* the bravura of Manet, the opened perspective of the then-sensational Japanese prints, all the "painterly" refinements are present. But what twists the wall at the left with such particular vehemence, and in what still-life or pose in frozen motion do those violent streaks across the window-pane, that is the absolute foreground, find reflection?

"In love with the natural image with the passion of my own image" – such might have been the artist's motto.* He will get closer to the hills, to the postman, and the pouting girl by using the new freedom of his vocabulary. Distortion will increase the perceived sensation, underline the anxious twist of flesh, accelerate the moving leg across the surface. The fields stay

*

"The axiom is this: 'People, let us love what we love'," Vincent wrote to his friend, the young painter Anton Ridder van Rappard in 1881.

flat as the heavy pigment stamps them on the weave of the linen, but they shoot into released distances as the artist watches from his window. Here it is perfectly justifiable to make the most far-fetched interpretations: that the low wall which cuts through this greyed pink landscape is van Gogh's symbol of a refusal to escape from the asylum; that he shows flight to be very easy, but will not plan it; and that the whole temptation of freedom is melancholy, as the prison of soft rain will always keep man from what he longs for. Or, contrariwise, that the wall makes no difference, it is not a barrier, but points the direction of escape; first one crosses a transverse path in the plowed field, then over the little obstacle, away from the hills and into a widening horizon, refreshed by the cooling sadness of pastel rain.

Admitted that the latter interpretation seems improbable, still it exists, as do many others, all relevant, because the forms demand continuous interpretation. Van Gogh's solution, an act of genius which still exerts a profound influence on contemporary artists, was to give emotional significance to the object even as it was being depicted. It is not a simple device, like painting a wall as you would build a wall, or even using a loose stroke for cumulus clouds, a tight one for a tooth. Rather, there is a negation of the freedom to paint as one pleases in order to use this freedom to fulfill an interior demand. Monet will knowingly twist a façade; van Gogh will twist the mind, and with Monet's pincers. Emotion finds equivalence in the substance of paint. Sometimes one element will dominate – and everyone, including the artist, recognizes a failure. But van Gogh must produce failures, both meaningless lumps of pigment and ludicrously cringing subjects, in order to find his expression. And it came off so often – so often that whole schools of artists could enter in his mystery, and see what they wanted to say as they wanted to say it. Still, van Gogh's masterpieces often elude them, for he opened most fully in front of such unpredictable objects as a Rembrandt engraving, or a vase full of irises, or the most casual view from his window of wide fields under a spring rain.

With Gauguin, the intellectual amateur, it is another matter. He saw the chinks in the armor of the Impressionists, perhaps because he was trained to see chinks all his life. This misanthropic, brilliant man-of-the-world recognizes that when Monet justified by scrupulous observation a crimson streak at 5:45 P.M. across the lower left segment of the rose window of the Rouen Cathedral, he meant he wanted to use some crimson in that area of the picture. Thus why not use crimson, or pure cerulean, or the brightest green wherever needed – or wherever possible? Bright color as wanted, and why not want it everywhere, advised Gauguin; and

shapes, too. If the landscape of *The Sacred Mountain* [fig. 42], 1882, needed an extra fillip at the corner, then push up the hill or a plant or bang an exotic fence across the foreground. Vincent van Gogh would calculate for hours, make meticulous pen drawings, and finally sense the point where the fullest use of paint and the fullest expression of subject intercept, then he would paint like a fury; Gauguin had the shortcut: pull out all the stops of the color organ, and work the form in; then, if it does not come off, find new motifs in the South Seas, in Brittany, any place where bulk and stylization offer flexibility of interpretation. In his paintings – and Gauguin had the supreme courage to live and die them – he considered the possibilities of absolute freedom: any art, any subject; all traditions, no responsibility, any passion, no unities, no perspective, any distance, any color, all risks, all knowledge, no reportage, no conventionality, no servility* – and he became a great man whose pictures have suffered from his glory.

Van Gogh fused subject with means, Gauguin emancipated all methods. Their followers, a small number at first, but always articulate, kept both their altars holy and accessible. By the end of the century a diffident Norwegian, Edvard Munch, had so quickly understood their premises that he decided to paint the pure interior landscape, with all the freedom of Gauguin and with all the commitment of van Gogh. In such large, dreamy pictures as *White Night* [fig. 43], 1901, and in some rather violent figure studies, Munch emancipated his rather academic techniques so that they might find appropriate vessels for anxiety. Most important, he brought back to the parlors of Northern and Central Europe the possibility of acting again in painting – of expressing the most private and the most precious ideals or

*

To borrow a locution from Mr. Barnett Newman.

Abstract painting

43 Edvard Munch

White Night, 1901

obsessions, of spilling into form all one's withheld loves and indrawn hates. Munch's own problem with his art, it seems to me, was his inclination to be rather lazy, not as a worker, for he left a mountain of canvases, but as an artist who used oil paint. He was satisfied with the easiest effects – notice the flaccid shadows on the snow in the middle-ground of *White Night,* or the curves of the waves. In freeing his technique he also impoverished it; no matter how vast a range of emotion it was asked to express, it always had to rely upon a very few effects. The artist's graphic work, in which he took a fine fanatical interest, shows no such thinness.

Munch was not only an important carrier of ideas and prophet of Expressionism, but, at the very beginning, his failures set an object lesson. It is not enough to be able to say anything in any manner, or to make a point as forcefully as possible; the whole creative process must change, and grow with the artist, or all his noblest violence will sound as softly as those painted armies that clash unseen in the basements of every academy in the world.

In Germany, in the first decade of this century, Kandinsky was quick to sense the possibilities of the new-born Expressionist program. Like van Gogh and Gauguin, he released his hand and his eye in front of nature, pushing the most vivid colors up hills and across fields until the painting becomes a moving river of pigment. Unlike van Gogh and Munch, however, Kandinsky's ecstasy is that of the level-headed artist; he neither identifies himself with the act of transforming the subject, nor attempts to visualize his longings, but methodically seeks the sensation of the landscape in the sensation of paint, and recognizes that by increasing the intensity of the latter, the electric charge of the former also rises. Some of his pictures in this period were subtitled *Improvisation,* suggesting that attachment to technique was at

44 Wassily Kandinsky

Landscape, 1911

least as strong as that to hills or trees*, and, indeed, in a few years the artist would leave the image of nature behind him forever. However, in such works as this 1911 *Landscape* [fig. 44], a notable point of balance was established between the line that expresses an upward surge and the hill that rises to the sky; between the thrusting vertical and the tree trunk; between the visual association and its sources in reality.

It remained, however, for a Central European who worked in Paris to bring Expressionism to its fullest and most inspired realization. Chiam Soutine came to France after the launching of Cubism, as van Gogh had arrived after Impressionism, and he faced a similar dilemma: finding a way to express the desperate fears, longings,

*

Kandinsky wrote in 1918: "When I tackled the landscape, it was with the feeling of advancing in battle against a foe. A foe, I may add, that in the end usually gained the upper hand . . ."

visions of glory, and expressions or negations of certainty with the elegant, eloquent vocabulary of modern art. Like van Gogh, he decided to fuse the creative act with the subject: the artist's sensation would unite the real object and the painted one in a new identity where sensation would have primacy. A more expert craftsman than van Gogh, which also acted as a handicap, for craftsmanship can obscure as well as facilitate, Soutine's pictorial vision was more limited. This, perhaps, was as much the fault of the time as the man, for van Gogh could always observe with the clear, astonished eye of the divinely protected discoverer, while Soutine was too accomplished an artist to find surprises – he had to struggle for them on some hot field or in an unheated room.

In his masterful landscape, *The Hill* [fig. 45], painted around 1919, I see the hill with a house on top, but below, and to the left, I find a hooknosed witch, a handkerchief tied around her head, holding the collar of a squatting dragon. But the beast's right side is defined by a dark area which now appears to be a curling-horned steer, drastically foreshortened, rising up to the farmhouse, while below, guarding his eyes with his forearm, a man tumbles backward into the sea. A few minutes later, I might have difficulty in finding some of these forms again. Perhaps the landscape will return, with all its roads, banks of trees, coils of earth, and flying clouds. But the very manipulation of pigment has pried the subject from nature into the personal sensation of terror, violence – and paint. Such a picture repays hours of examination, for it is fitted together as deftly as any Cubist portrait. Interweaving layers of hue, coiled lines that shoot and cage motion within the rectangle, an elaborate play of tonalities up and down the image, all suggest spontaneity, but also disclose the patience and the labor involved. That the landscape is filled with animal energy, at times sinister, at times benevolently pastoral, is a logical projection of Soutine's vision. Everything in the painting breathes and devours space and color. Nature is again populated with demigods who re-sanctify their ancient myths under the most banal fields or within everyday trees.

Like van Gogh, Soutine must produce failures, and must run the risk of boring or too quickly satiating some cultivated tastes. Being honest to his search for the sensation of the object, he must recognize that a bad picture can sometimes come off in these terms as well as a good one. But he is a persuasive reminder to artists of his generation and to the following one (he would be only in his late fifties if he were living today) that with the help of fury and dedication one can seal the mysteries of nature within the mysteries of paint, and that the human subject can enter a painting through many different doors.

Oskar Kokoschka, also a Central European, but never a Parisian, was an Expressionist before Sou-

tine and continues to be one. His first mature works, strange, disease-haunted portraits, were considerably influenced by Munch, and have a power and hypnotic intensity which elevate them to the peaks of contemporary art. In *The Crab* [fig. 46], 1940-41, there is the same vigorous splashing and turning of paint on canvas that has been the characteristic of Expressionism since van Gogh. Forms are distorted to increase their natural action; the claws are more clawing, the rocks more jagged. The strange, menacing crab faces the swimmer, the sea, and the castle with impassive hostility; he is vast in the foreground (and a piece of rope to his left suggests that he is, indeed, about three feet high).

But something is wrong – the scene is set too carefully, like a long-discussed and plotted design with its pat symbolism and backdrop reminiscent of a painting of a painting. This is the final dilemma of the Expressionist – how to make "Art" out of the sensation. The answer seems obvious – pick up where Munch left off, work hard at techniques, balance each tone, paint "abstractly" so forms will run nicely into their neighbors and the edge of the picture will curve the eye back towards the central drama. But an artist cannot manufacture style, and there are no applicable secrets of the trade. Munch's very preoccupation with what he was saying and how precisely he was expressing it had to distract him from any idea of method. Kokoschka became diverted by style, and the banal little curl of paint that is supposed to be a cloud and also a grace note marks the spot at which his art founders. The rhetorical statement, with its obvious subterfuges and its promises of success, is the temptation; its existence was implicit in the earliest beginnings of Expressionism. As soon as such artists stop betting their whole lives on the validity of the sensation, and look about for corroboration within craft, then they admit sensation does not justify itself. The artist

45 Chiam Soutine

The Hill, ca. 1919

Abstract painting

46 Oskar Kokoschka

The Crab, 1940-41

becomes the impresario of his own dramas – a backer instead of a creator – and can no longer be indifferent to success or failure.

In the tranquil but vehemently flaming landscapes of Matisse and Bonnard the tortured duality of object and subject do not exist – still no discussion of Expressionism could be complete without their presence and authority. These are no sensitized Central Europeans, but Frenchmen – Parisians, with all the superb confidence and ability to compromise and negotiate which the title suggested. At about the same time as Munch, Matisse recognized the contributions of Cézanne van Gogh, Gauguin, and Seurat – not as liberations and exalted promises, but as additional links to the chain of France's history of art. In *The Terrace, St. Tropez* [fig. 47], painted about 1904, the artist's wife sits quietly knitting while sunlight, flowers, bushes, and trees, all about her, burst into the most intense colors. Gauguin ad-

vised using a pure blue if one was going to use blue, and Seurat broke surfaces into contrasting dots of brightness. But it remained for Matisse and his fellow Fauves (the group was aptly nicknamed "wild beasts" by one of those many French art critics who always have opportunely put their feet in their mouths) to find a way to construct a picture that would exalt brightness in all its purity. Matisse found the form that sustains a red flower against a green leaf. Curving, loosened undulations and brisk twists at the points; a willingness to commit the picture to its patterns – note the cascade of leaves from the upper left corner – and, finally, an uninhibited praise of painting and its difficulties, such were some of the stratagems the artist employed. With all the assurance of a master, he throws into the sky an arbitrary diagonal from the roof of the house to the top center of the painting, letting the tree act as a bare structure in its relationship to the building and as a

47 Henri Matisse

The Terrace, St. Tropez, ca. 1904

carrier of green across the image. A plant will emerge from the horizon, brandishing sea-serpent mustaches; a swinging branch will tentatively accuse the seated figure, but the violence is only that of a hot summer day – and the brilliance inherent in creating a masterpiece. Matisse is not searching; he is exercising a master's prerogatives.

The clarity and inevitable rightness of his forms become a way of painting almost as soon as they are defined. The artist exposes the solid construction of his picture with a pride similar to Cézanne's, but with even greater confidence that there are no weak spots. The line from Impressionism is not only revitalized with new strength and justification, but a philosophy of bold and joyous action projects it into the future. The courage of Matisse is not in the heavy sweep of a brush or in ecstatically bringing off the twist of form that corresponds so perfectly with a twist of the spirit. There is a continual action of hesitancy in his painting – the final shape is left on the canvas after a settling down of approximations, after small strokes are ordered into agreement. Sensibility is polished and sharpened to calculate each nuance, to retreat before each possible difficulty, and to exploit the slightest advantage. The result is a boldness of conception and completeness of execution that has galvanized painters for forty years. The purpose of his art, Matisse once proudly stated, is to be as comfortable as an armchair; a French poet has seen it function for Baudelaire's "luxury, calm, and voluptuousness." But neither indications of purpose and effect seem to give sufficient emphasis to the absorption of emotion, painter's and spectators' alike, in the brilliant hues of the Fauve canvasses. The exposed nerves and lacerated flesh of a van Gogh or a Soutine seem unnecessarily tragic, or eloquent, in the face of this sunny porch in France before World War I. Still, the Northerners were always able to avoid the perils of

Abstract painting

empty decoration and trivial good taste – traps for the self-satisfied or success-seeking artist. Matisse himself in some benign "Nice Period" odalisques, and hundreds of his followers and colleagues, would not always be so fortunate.

It is perhaps irreverent to group the luminous compositions which Pierre Bonnard made of Southern France's trees, flowers, hills, and sea with the Expressionists. This artist is usually labeled a wonderful Impressionist who somehow kept living in the 1940's. But Bonnard, too, was haunted by the sensation, and became an Expressionist of pleasure – as great and heroic a position as is being one of pain.

Unlike Kandinsky, he does not play with the landscape or tease it into battle, although like that Russian-born artist he was keenly alert to every possibility the picture presented as it grew in correspondence to nature. Unlike Matisse and the Cubists, he does not reveal the skeleton beneath the paint, but hides it so carefully that it has remained invisible even to many of his most enthusiastic admirers. A series of interlocking ovals and softened bends roll into curves that gently move up the surface of the canvas. Bonnard's contrived structure reinforces the symbols of biological growth. Spectacular color conceals plots of tone which wind into every area, like the most delicate spider web, until the whole work is finally enmeshed in a secret unity. And hues, too, which seem so capriciously varied by the overwhelming presence of flowering hills, are circumspectly locked in the body of the image.

The sensation of beauty in nature – which also carries the connotations of evanescence and loss – was so powerful for the painter that he constantly had to dilute it with modesty and informality. Only in some ambitious studies of nudes and in a handful of large allegorical landscapes with figures did Bonnard attempt to assert that his vision was nobler than himself, and these, on the whole, were failures. In his many triumphs, such as *The Riviera* [fig. 48], 1928, the artist offers an instantaneous glimpse of the sensation, and then, as one studies the painting, the recreation of the entire acceptance of beauty is revealed. Each bush and field must be fragmented so that it cannot impose a false proclamation of dominating grandeur; all elements must be raised to identical importance and perfection of finish (which is reminiscent of Monet, but that dedicated experimenter reduced all parts to an anonymity that he hoped would facilitate the entrance of art – which it did, but for Seurat and Picasso more than for Monet). Bonnard's colors and tones are all partially sacrificed to their neighbors to bring about the final, explosive fusion of nature and Bonnard within the frame. What else were van Gogh and Soutine doing?

The Hollander and the Pole, in French exile, battered and broke in through the front door; Bonnard, like a welcome son, walked in the back way. Superficially he used the opposite of their means – quiet and uncertain withdrawal instead of shouting, courageous attack. But all three saw in nature their personal and elevated ideals. Note that all were especially drawn to commonplace subjects – a pair of worn shoes or a cheap chair and an old pipe for van Gogh; a hotel bellhop or a limp, butcher-shop duck for Soutine; the after-lunch clutter of crockery or the incidental glance at a book for Bonnard. Exploring the interior landscape, they see the glimmerings of new worlds which they then proceed to invent in lifetimes of passionate intensity. The broken, flickering gardens of Bonnard have had as great an impact as the twisting cypresses of van Gogh, and it is not surprising to find younger artists attempting to plant one within the other.

Art history is not a chain or a tree or a river, but simply and intricately the history of all mankind.

48 Pierre Bonnard

The Riviera, 1928

Abstract painting

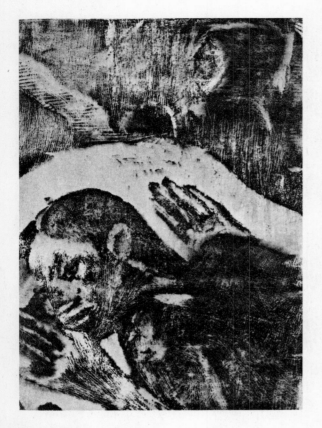

49 Paul Gauguin

Manao Tupapao
(*Watched by the Spirit of the Dead*),
ca. 1893-95

The tendencies toward and of abstract painting and Expressionism may be the most important movements in the art of the first half of our century, and the most relevant ones to more recent developments. Still, every other sort of painting and attempt to paint co-exists with them, influencing them to or away from certain positions. The periphery is also vital. An academician in 1910 who still is so true to his great master, Ingres, that he must also ostentatiously cloak his face whenever he passes through a room containing a Delacroix, expresses the importance of his profession as pungently as Picasso meeting Apollinaire at the café of the moment. A complete genius may come out of nowhere, like Henri Rousseau, and only after his magisterial presence is known do we recognize a whole new tribe of his friends and relations. Or a desire may be so strong that it will continually, and convincingly, erupt through the most carefully laid plans to circumvent it.

In the following six paintings [figs. 49 to 54] one can see the powerful grip of the fantastic on a great part of modern expression. Here the motive for painting is almost destroyed in its process, and with a certain pleasure, as if by offering up the prerogative of art as a sacrifice, the desired nightmare will take fuller possession of the dreamer. The subject, veiled with verbal metaphors, returns to haunt certain artists. And it is almost invariably to the most intellectual painters that the fantastic subject has made its visitation.

Gauguin, as we have seen, was led to the Gordian knot of technique and cut through it suavely and easily. Still, there had to be things to paint worthy of his new freedom, and this artist must travel to find them, for they would not appear outside his window or at the dinner table. As did the Romantic poets, he felt a need for distance in space, a remove from denying home to an unfamiliar culture, with a sea voyage, a noble cause,

50 James Ensor

Magic Musicians, 1891

and an ending on the crescendo notes of ironic heroism. The Byronic myth captured the French imagination more sharply than it ever did England's: Isidore Ducasse, for instance, had to become the Count of Lautréamont, and he often claimed, perhaps with a certain hope of reassuring prospective publishers, that his *Maldoror* was merely an extension of Byron. Gauguin's voyage ends in a primitive Erewhon – among stiff archaic carvings by Breton peasants and pot-bellied idols worshipped by honey-skinned athletes in the Marquesas. In *Manao Tupapao* (*Watched by the Spirit of the Dead*) [fig. 49], a woodcut made around 1893-95, the stark-eyed nightmare is as much the artist's as the subject's. The hooded figure, with the pointed nose and sanctimoniously drooping mouth of a vaudeville cleric, materializes behind the girl. She stares straight ahead. The grain of the wood-block becomes the fog between asleep and awake, and the white arc of the bed,

the line between the reality of the heroine and the dream that will kill her. This is not a tourist's observation or a rationale of psychosomatics, but an attempt to believe in and to evoke the supernatural. Gauguin's quizzical Gallic stare becomes hypnotized by the meanings it sought in form. Sophisticated plays of white and black reassure us that the artist is still present, but he no longer builds a scene, he has become the Ancient Mariner.

In his more complicated pictures, fascinated by shining lavenders and crimsons and vegetal patterns, Gauguin remained the detached and exploring artist, bringing back, sooner or later, to those who would understand, in Paris, the novel possibilities offered by a liberated technique. His influence was considerable, and almost immediate, for he demonstrated that primitive cultures were an ideal source of supply and amusement. He found his impacts ready-made – a prefabri-

Abstract painting

51 Giorgio de Chirico

Disturbing Journey, 1913

cated intensity to match the probable potential of the means. Gauguin's discoveries were bound to be attractive; amateurs, geniuses, and hacks have been looting museums and archeological expeditions ever since. But if this was his influence, his contribution was made in the very act of surrendering himself to a force he sought to cultivate as a hobby. Gouging into the wood, and making the most of the detachment his medium gave him, the artist was willing to become the recorder of unfathomable human feeling. The artist steps aside, and the vision of death is caught in open eyes which are not planned as areas of blackness in a composition of darks and lights.

Ensor of Belgium also found a fantastic world to record, but he saw it in his own house; his voyage is around the bedroom, or, at most, along Brussels' main street. Not committed to any avant-garde or program, as Gauguin was, he could adapt with satisfied provincialism the dis-

coveries of Impressionism and Post-Impressionism a few decades after the fact. And he could devote himself to keeping alive the cheerful, secular demons of the North – always using the best possible tools invented by others, plus his own homemade instruments, which were extremely ingenious. *Magic Musicians* [fig. 50], 1891, whistle and pluck at their instruments. A bird uses a bird's skull for castanets, fish grow claws to play the bass or hold a clarinet. Flying and swimming, pinching and pecking, they chorus the happy terrors of Bosch and Brueghel where nightmares are invoked only to be dismissed with ridicule.

Gauguin like de Chirico, Ernst, Klee, and Picasso, brings the fantastic to spotlighted stages, making it public, articulate, and influential. Ensor, like Redon – and one might even include Ryder in this category – avoids the highways, follows his own path in the provinces, and constructs a private treasury of living Mardi Gras

52 Max Ernst

The Forest, 1928

masks, strutting skeletons, and all the paraphernalia of a comic dance of death. An unwanted vocabulary is kept fresh and lively for future generations, and for his contemporaries there is a masterful sideshow, sometimes scornful, sometimes ingratiating, but always proudly insistent on the dignity and value of eccentricity.

Ensor achieved international recognition after the taste for the fantastic had been established; de Chirico was one of the inventors of the taste. Starting as a local malcontent with the abstract direction modern art in general, and Futurism in particular, were taking – a role he has since tried to inflate to operatic proportions – in the second decade of the century this Greek-born Italian was able to materialize an imagery of dreams, enigmas, and obsessive hallucinations. He made his private world public poetry – exploding the perspective of the Renaissance masters into steep, wheeling ramps; conceiving light as a source for

gelatinous shadows and space as an ever-receding horizon. The little train chugging off, the empty square, arcades filled with darkness, the terrifying caprice of the monumental tower, the comfortable nostalgia of leave-takings, the abandoned platform, and the passive brutality of family gods – these were some of de Chirico's most famous images. In *Disturbing Journey* [fig. 51], 1913, the success of the mystery seems due, as much as anything, to the artist's informal treatment of his repertory of symbols like an element of the painter's technique – as de Hooch used his figures and courtyards. The locomotive that seems about to crash through a brick wall is arrested in its motion by the strange waxy light that fill this labyrinth of piers and arches, just as the foreboding darkness of the central core of space is kept enigmatic by the contrasting, and pictorially stabilizing, glow it emits. De Chirico dedicates his mystery to paint, and is rewarded by its embodiment

79

Abstract painting

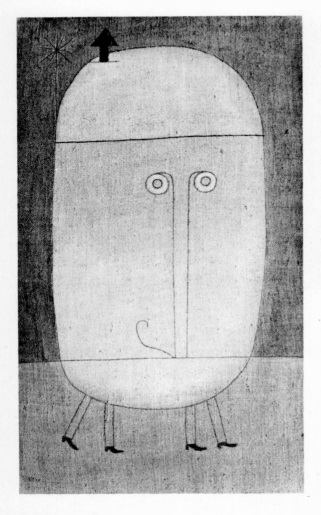

53 Paul Klee

Mask of Fear, 1932

on the surface of the canvas. Later, when he painted simply for the mystery's sake, and, still later, simply for paint's sake, he produced monstrous banalities of sunny horses and fat fruit. There may be a certain vulgarity in *Disturbing Journey,* a sort of Hollywood pleasure in instant effects. But in de Chirico's successful pictures – and this is one of the best of them – such weaknesses are a source of strength, for only under the cover of an instant effect can the artist make his subtle, marginal additions of enigma, and finally arrive at a modern recreation of the fantastic.

Although de Chirico did his notable early work almost completely independent of any movement, his pictures were quickly recognized by the Paris Surrealists as being ideal illustrations for their literature, a field in which this painter is also extremely able. In revolt against what seemed to be the materialist program of modern – i. e. abstract and Post-Impressionist – art and prosperous capitalism they insisted that a mystery should be the most easily ascertainable element of painting. A Cubist Picasso might be more profoundly ambiguous and disturbing than a 1913 de Chirico, but it never attempts to make its riddles quite so apparent. For Max Ernst, a glance at a painting should be sufficient to arouse uneasiness – at the very least. *The Forest* [fig. 52], 1928, looms and glooms at the spectator after the briefest introduction. Further examination might increase bewilderment, for, like most Surrealists, Ernst delights in elaborate tricks and unconventional effects. Devices of "frottage" (basically, the rubbing a child can make with pencil from a coin under a piece of paper), decalcomania, spattering pigment through stencils or over templates, these and many other methods can act in two successfully Surrealist ways: they stimulate the artist's imagination while he works and lead him to the unexpected which he seeks so earnestly, and they also increase the desired mystifications.

54 Pablo Picasso

Night Fishing at Antibes, 1939

As far as many of the Surrealist painters were concerned, such a program led to clever illustrations which today, only a decade or two later, already have the prim look of Victorian gewgaws. A few, however, Ernst included, were artists enough to be Surrealistically Surreal. They profited by an added freedom of means and an eager, avant-garde atmosphere to work as they pleased. Heightening abstract form with carefree colors or delighting in the increasingly complicated references to multiple images and metaphysical notions, they ignored dreams and manifestoes, and wrote one more vivid chapter to the history of the International School of Paris. Still, the manifestoes did appear, and Breton wrote them magnificently. Salvador Dali (who was later excommunicated from the movement and rechristened, as a parting gesture, "Avida Dollars") made a sensation in New York by wearing a stuffed pink brassière to a party and boasting that

he liked to put pork chops on his wife's bare shoulder. Fantastic art was the vogue. Instead of being produced by solitary mystics and visionaries, it was ordered by ballet backers, perfume bottlers, and window-display designers.

Private inspiration for the fantastic, however, was by no means dead. The Swiss-German Paul Klee found in the tradition of Cubism, and in the archaeological example of Gauguin – and also in the works of such late German Romantics as Klimt – a new handwriting for primitive subjects. Colors, shapes, their arrangements, the rough surfaces and arbitrary hues of *Mask of Fear* [fig. 53], 1932, could all be termed abstract, except, perhaps, for the four neat little black shoes. Yet they are fastened together into a ponderous totem with prophetic television antenna and a dark, protruding arrow (note, by the way, if one blocks out the arrow, how completely pictorial its role is seen to be; it suggests wounds or aggression, but

Abstract painting

55 Joseph Stella

Battle of Light, Coney Island, 1913

it also keeps the whole composition from sagging badly at the top). The components of Klee's picture are conceived as abstractions in order to sustain an exploring fancy and humor. This involves dealing with the fantastic with laboratory methods: finding which line will suggest most succinctly an apprehensive stare, which colors help fish to fly, or a cat change into a flower. Like Matisse and Miró, Klee is not afraid of the urgency and directness of infantile expression, but he refined its forms and gestures even further than they, insisting on the "art" of each detail and its subordination to the planned drama of the picture.

One of the most prolific of modern painters, his laboratory system permitted Klee to coin an endless variety of images and methods. If in this process of exhausting the inspiration – bringing the tiniest of sketches to a complete statement of taste, including a careful job of matting and an

inspired one of titling – the range of mood and even stature is consciously restricted; nevertheless, he succeeded in making the fantastic a product of abstraction. Scrupulously avoiding the grand manner and the spontaneous passage, he prods the cube into a comic jig or transforms it into a bittersweet flight of petals.

Only Picasso or Miró could give the fantastic a monumental scale, and only Picasso could do it and keep the easy shock that had so intrigued the Surrealists. In *Night Fishing at Antibes* [fig. 54], 1939, the real world and the painter's mix and jumble into a painter's construction wherein a whole new race is born. The girl at the right holding her bicycle and licking what appears to be a double ice-cream cone; her friend with the lantern; the two fishermen, one staring at a fish, and the fish staring back; the stars tumbling among the rocks; have all the mystery and magic that many realists seek among totems and tabus.

56 Morgan Russell

To Form Synchromy, Number 4, 1914

Here Cubism consciously embraces all styles, retaining the faceting of an arm even as it presents monsters and poetry. Abstraction becomes a way to all goals.

There is, of course, no guarantee attached. In fact, compared with Picasso's masterpieces, *Night Fishing at Antibes* is not an impressive achievement – there is nothing wrong with the idea, but its execution seems relaxed to a damaging degree. However, by the late thirties, before the sealing-off of France under Nazi occupation, Cubism, Expressionism, Surrealism, with all the individual variations that made up these directions, were rapidly merging, and painters, with Picasso in the lead, worked toward styles that would have the authority of the first, the emotional intensity of the second, and the personal liberty of the third. Many, as has been indicated, tried to mix self-contained effects – as the sixteenth-century Mannerists had attempted to make a cocktail of Venetian color and Florentine form; with equally eclectic results. A painter cannot simply decide to take advantage of a historical situation and "become" its logical projection, even though he sees that it is bound to happen. How such a fusion has taken place in America will be considered in the final section of this book.

Such, briefly, is the background in Paris.

America has its history, at home and abroad, and it is of considerable importance to the story.

The pictures by Joseph Stella, Morgan Russell, and Max Weber [figs. 55 to 57] are representative of the "first wave" of abstract painting, U.S.A. Stella, who worked in Italy and France from 1909 to 1912, was an accepted member of the Futurist movement. Russell, with MacDonald-Wright, founded a splinter manifesto-movement in Paris, Synchronism, just before the first World War – much to the disgust of Delaunay who felt the invaders had stolen his colored discs. Weber was

57 Max Weber

Rush Hour, New York, 1915

one of the very first Americans to meet the avant-gardes in Paris, where he arrived in 1905; by 1908 he had attended classes in Matisse's short-lived school and had become one of the first to recognize the genius of Henri Rousseau. With them, and such artists as Walkowitz, Maurer, Hartley, Dove, and, of course, John Marin, the American art world made firm contact with the Fauves and Cubists almost as soon as they appeared. The salons of Gertrude Stein in Paris and the galleries of the eminent photographer Alfred Stieglitz in New York also solidly linked both cities together. However, knowing what is going on is not even half the battle. Most of these American painters (the most important exception is Marin, and he went on to a highly personal style from studies of Cézanne and Whistler), elated with modernity, proceeded to paint it just as they had painted a straight landscape or figure-piece a few years before. The repeated tops of merry-go-rounds and arcs of roller-coasters that fill Stella's *Battle of Light, Coney Island* [fig. 55], 1913, are modelled and tinted like any conventional apple; the small embellishments and careful decorations obtruding from focal points of the composition show how little the artist understood that abstract forms can exist as functioning elements in a painting. Russell's *To Form Synchromy, Number 4* [fig. 56], 1914, while completely devoid of recognizable shapes, is simply a background of angles, constructed in realist space, upon which the artist can place the hues he is so interested in – illuminating a red next to a yellow from an arbitrary source of light, much as Harnett might have, had he been interested in color. Weber's *Rush Hour, New York* [fig. 57], 1915, takes the angles of fragmented architecture, makes them open and close across the composition, and then presents them as if the artist had copied some wonderful, imaginary mechanical fan. All that they took from the excitement of

58 Stuart Davis

The President, 1922

Paris was new subject matter, which they might have found while painting the Grand Canyon, or Balinese dancers. A remarkable skill in adapting these shifting transparencies to home-bred vision is evident, and American Cubists, Non-Objectivists, Expressionists, Surrealists, etc., almost invariably uphold our nation's reputation for enterprising ingeniousness. They respect "Art," paint lovingly and patiently, are filled with new ideas for arrangements and effects – skyscrapers would look well Cubistically, or New England churches, and the huge factories, and, for that matter, the political and moral problems of a proletariat. Still, this was only another way to present the subject, and as soon as the surprise faded most of them abandoned it. Perhaps they felt constrained by the need for making dramas work in visible structures, or by the very limitation of subject matter, as they conceived it, which the Cubist point of view demanded. Stella, after a notable series of semi-Futurist depictions of Brooklyn Bridge, went on to a tight realist style of peacocks, chaste profiles, and gold backgrounds; Russell also turned to a private brand of Neo-Classicism, filled with Roman architecture and symbolic landscape; Weber painted rabbis, shaggy trees, and comfortable gatherings of ladies, in various manners – his eye cocked toward Paris – in a sensitive, anecdotal idiom. Wright took up Buddhist symbolism; Hartley looked to the obviously virile countryside; Maurer, in interludes between Cubist studies, relaxed in portraits of nostalgic, adolescent girls. It is interesting to note how many of these artists fled to some hermetic symbolism after the Cubist dissillusionment; perhaps they felt that now they must sacrifice everything to a meaning they could trust blindly, to a ritual and initiation. They would look back on Cubism as a sort of art-school discipline – which, for them, unfortunately, it was.

All this does not imply failure, but rather un-

Abstract painting

59 Alfred Maurer

Still-life with Pears, ca. 1931

derlines the superficial understanding, no matter how enthusiastic, America had with the beginnings of abstract art in Paris. Only a few men realized what was going on; the best known of them is Stuart Davis, who belongs to the generation after the first Americans in modern Paris. Already a trained and accomplished painter when he came into contact with Cubism, Davis quickly understood that it was not some new method for old materials, but rather a growth of different forms which demands a corresponding growth from every aspect of technique. His *The President* [fig. 58], 1922, sets buildings and plants, cut in panes like those of leaded glass, in a landscape of color. Variations of textures, as lights are brushed over darks; of interval and angle; of the interpenetrating lines themselves as they disappear or change tone, all endow the painting with its own flowers and buildings, with its own controlled play or space, back and forth, up and down the canvas. Yankee ingeniousness is present, but here it works with the picture, not on it. A certain bland severity might mar somewhat the final effect, but a leadership for abstract painting in America is assured.

After its initial contacts with Paris, and the appearance of such enterprising phenomena as the 1913 Armory Show; *Vanity Fair* magazine, under the cultural guidance of Frank Crowninshield; Henry McBride's art criticism in the *Sun* (Gertrude Stein used to boast to astonished Parisians that she could get the still-anathematized Matisse a full page in one of New York's leading dailies, just by passing the word on to Mr. McBride); as well as the arrival of such artists as Marcel Duchamp and Picabia during World War I; the formation of great collections of modern art by Dr. Albert Barnes, A. E. Gallatin, Walter Arensberg, Katherine Dreier, and many others; and the establishment of the Museum of Modern

60 Arthur Dove

The Brothers, 1941

Art in New York, abstract art became as American as baseball or Archibald MacLeish. Every sort of person and institution was attracted to it, for every sort of reason. For cultists it became a cult; for formalists a system of "significant" or "plastic" form, etc.; those who were preoccupied with narrative details found a new excuse to bring them to unparalleled levels of illustration by reacting "against" abstraction; indeed, for the defenders of a Benton or a Cadmus, a major justification is the negative claim that they are not "empty," like the "decadent" French Cubists.

Paris, of course, was the fountainhead. A book published there in 1932, *Artistes Americains de Paris,* lists thirty-eight leading members of the group (among those still active are: George Baer, Paul Burlin, John Cox, Emlen Etting, Vincent Glinsky, John Graham, Lee Hersch, Hilaire Hiler, Carl Holty, Sidney Laufman, Isidore Levy, Oronzio Maldarelli, Anna Neagoe, Walter Pach,

Abraham Rattner, Ary Stillman, Vaclav Vytlacil, and Jean Xceron). Practically every American painter over forty has been at some time a citizen of the Left Bank – not a tourist there, as are the swarms of Fulbright scholars and "G. I. Bill" students who have courageously re-made Paris of the 1950's in their own image. The French intellectual of today, who reads Faulkner, Miller, Hemingway, and, perhaps, Henry James, who applauded *"Un Tramway Nommé Désire,"* translated by Cocteau and starring Arletty, will overhear controversies concerning "bop" versus Armstrong, or Léger versus Kandinsky in his favorite café, conducted by a new class of bohemians who hardly bother to learn French.

In the late twenties and thirties, along with the Depression and the dominance of a social realist school, European abstract styles had original and personal continuations in America. Provincial manners were evolved – with all the excellent and

Abstract painting

61 Karl Knaths

The Moon, 1950

limiting connotations the term "provincial" implies. Alfred Maurer, in his little studio in New York, worked out such delicate, lacy variations of Cubism as *Still-life with Pears* [fig. 59], around 1932. The awkwardness, which is of the mind, not the hand, for Maurer was a prodigy in the Sargentesque idiom, lends a certain individual charm. Note how the white block jumps into the picture from the right and collides with a dark pear while changing the color of the one below, or how the line of another cube cuts across the bowl of fruit. The devices of Cubism are elaborated, exalted, and finally become a second protagonist in the drama – a sort of anti-fruit hero in the picture. But by hanging his still-life between its appearance in reality and an idealized mechanism of interpenetrating cubes which have palpable volume, Maurer created a conflict of his own whose resolution in paint is excellent, if minor art. The disturbing smell of the studio is

apt to be sensed rather strongly in this artist's work; he not only reveals the act of creation, but also the amount of sweat that went into it. But exquisite, artificial balances finally come off, and give Maurer's picture their flavor. Although he had to keep reverting, over and over again, to wish-fulfillment depictions of Italianate dream-girls, he would always return to his battle for the ideal form that could both support nature and be independent in it.

Maurer's method was to qualify the natural image; Arthur G. Dove's was to find a way to accept it completely. Unlike Soutine, who would identify the whole business of painting with his whole vision of a landscape, Dove sought equivalents of nature in forms that, *a priori,* would be abstract. The Indian village landscape of *The Brothers* [fig. 60], 1941, is reminiscent of ectoplasmic manifestations photographed during a seance. In searching for a pantheist currency of

62 Stuart Davis

Report from Rockport, 1940

shapes, Dove always ran the danger of being banal – making the soaring form soar too glibly; or a squatting curve is given so animalistic a contour that it resembles a Walt Disney dwarf. Still, in his pursuit of the abstract picture while lovingly investigating the world, Dove also found a tranquil and eccentric beauty; tranquil because of the calm affection with which he viewed each cow or mountain; eccentric because he pushed the tradition to such a personal – one might even call it "narrow minded" – pictorial viewpoint that it often was lost in private allusions. The results may be merely stenographic notes of one man's secret feelings or may be inflated, evangelical tracts.

With Karl Knath's œuvre, the provincial point of view becomes a cosmopolitan extension in another country. The space and color of Cubism, the evocative calligraphy of Klee, Matisse's swiftly meditative disposition of forms, European culture as such is absorbed and metamorphosed in the art of this Milwaukee-born Cape Codder. *The Moon* [fig. 61], 1950, is a daydream of shining darkness. The artist contrives each detail – the broken ladder, clapboard walls, wagon wheels – to fit the climax of light caught in branches, as dogs turn in fascination and barns settle on the pasture like pyramids. This is a refinement and dilution of Paris to suit America. Things are made a little easier pictorially, black lines guide the eye to each emphatic passage. There is a loss, as in a translation from French to English, and there is the gain of a new personality. Perhaps most important, there is the successful transplanting of Paris to Provincetown, Mass.

In *Report from Rockport* [fig. 62], 1940, and the two paintings by Arthur B. Carles [figs. 63 and 64], the background of Paris begins to fade away. Davis, who in a year knew Paris inside-out,

Abstract painting

63 Arthur B. Carles

Turkey, 1927

returned to the American scene not because it was American but because he was here. He finds in its abstraction a whole new capering set of shapes that, breaking free from clouds or gas pumps, energize the picture with their own velocity. As in the Cubists' collages, lettering is given back its independence as a string of magical signs; it spells "GARAGE" or whistles down a street as it wills. The artist finds new terms in the most trivial advertisements and exuberantly beats out the picture with them. Thick paint is kept in tight control, coarsening extremities and cutting curves into angles. Perspective and scale remain conventional, but can operate only on instructions from the heavy pipes, stars, and squiggles that keep to the surface of the picture. There is nothing provincial in the authority of these rhythms. Arp, Miró, and Picasso make their appearance, but they are treated as equals and add to the enjoyment of the *Report*.

Carles, for years an influential teacher in Philadelphia (whose students can always be recognized for their knowing use of burnt reds, warm greys, and fragile, horizontal compositions), also understood Paris and was able to go on from it to his own style. In such pictures as *Turkey* [fig. 63], 1927, and *Painting* [fig. 64], 1935-40, Carles prophetically exploited the ambiguities of abstract form. Color burns about the wings and body of the bird in the earlier picture, receding and advancing until the whole painting surrenders to its pulse – then the carefully drawn legs assert themselves again, and paint reverts to its given position. The bright wing, the mysterious ovoid that sweeps down from the top right corner, the receding textures, from the bird back to the left, all pour space in and out of the image until that action dominates, at which point the turkey returns to freeze attention. *Painting* uses similar means, but there is no home-base in reality. Rather the play of forms passes along

64 Arthur B. Carles

Painting, 1935-40

lines until certain elements obtrude, like the outlined circles appearing through the window-shape at the top right, or the dark jagged teeth at the bottom center. Action involves so many associations with form that each element retains its independence, but still invites associations. An unfamiliar note is sounded, related to Paris but unknown to it; within the tradition but different. And, fittingly, at some point during the execution of Carles's *Painting*, while Paris was lost, or in exile, the international styles of abstract art found new roots in this country.

Part three

Foreground and New York

Here reigned the dashing and all-fusing
spirit of the West, whose type is the
Mississippi itself, which, uniting the
streams of the most distant and opposite
zones, pours them along, helter-skelter,
in one cosmopolitan and confident tide.
Herman Melville, *The Confidence Man*

Almost simultaneously with the concept of a
United States of America came the demand for
its expression as a new cultural force. A re-
juvenated Athens in Boston, Massachusetts, or
even Athens, Georgia, was ringingly predicted by
friendly poets, sculptors, critics, and painters.
Until shocked by the unfamiliar myths of hard
work and industrialization, Europe considered
America a place where Continental ideals could
find extension and triumphant culmination on
rich farmlands and in communities devoted to
reason and to men's rights. Coleridge's "Panti-
socracy" was to flourish in the brave new world;
Washington is a frequent hero in early Romantic poetry; Franklin – D. H. Lawrence's materialist villain – was literally crowned by the more
influential beauties of the Bourbon court. With
such peremptory overtures, an American School
was bound to appear, and, fulfilling the bargain,
it was national – typically American – and mainly
successful in the degree that it found useful inspiration from European sources. In Munich,
Paris, Düsseldorf, or Rome, nineteenth-century
Yankees learned their lessons, discovered their
aptitudes, and proceeded to paint Americanly,
even as they thought, talked, dressed, and
breathed. The result was a fascinating series of
more or less original, parochial schools and
provincial giants whose histories have a con-

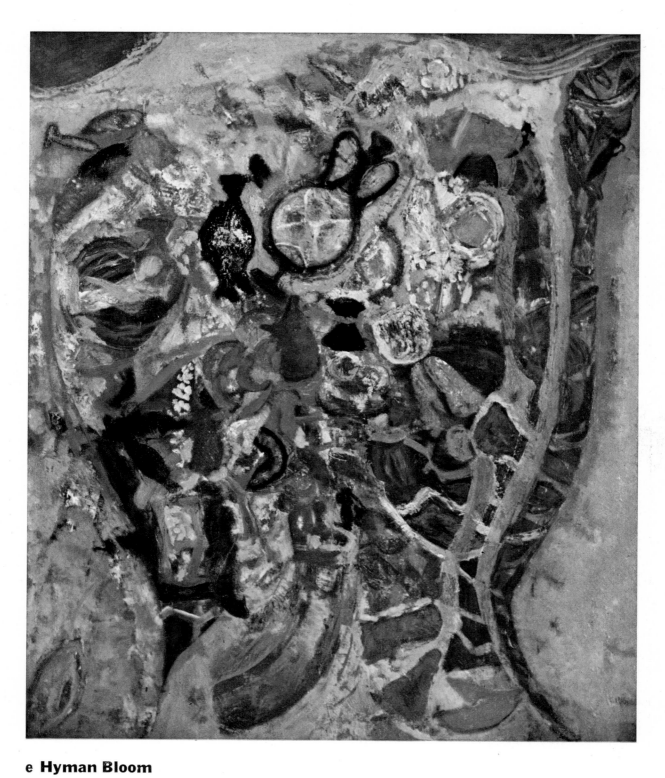

e Hyman Bloom

Archaeological Treasure, 1945

f Bradley Walker Tomlin

Number 7, 1950

g Robert Motherwell

The Poet, 1947, collage

95

h **Willem de Kooning**

Ashville, 1949

tinuity and logic roughly parallel to corresponding (but not necessarily contemporaneous) tendencies in Europe. Fire in a Bingham, Earl, Eakins, Ryder, Cole, Homer, or Whistler has its unique intensity and distinctive glow. Still, the escape into ingeniousness and hermitlike eccentricity; the sometimes furtive, sometimes affirmative dependence upon experiments abroad, and, most of all, the self-conscious selection of a school to belong to – all such characteristic handicaps of peripheral art – appear in even the best products of the American School.

One painter would become Barbizon; another adopt the brittle, polished manner which the Germans had found suitable to their Romanticism; most would take out naturalization papers for their pictorial ideas by painting the national subject – the incredible cliffs of the western mountains, the cozy meanders of the Hudson Valley, or buffalo hunters, or skyscrapers, or a baseball game. When the creative personality, the subject, and the makeshift style fused in a give-and-take of insight and affectionate labor, the pictures produced were as good as Eakins' tight-skinned rowers or Ryder's cloud-wandering moons. But when any one element dominated – especially when the painter became ambitiously artistic – the results were apt to be merely rhetorical doctrine and boring.

By the turn of the century, and the international recognition of Paris' hegemony in painting, the problem for the American artist was considerably simplified. He, too, could be international, like the Spanish Picasso, the Russian Chagall, or the Italian Modigliani. Instead of eclecticism, he could choose to be Paris. The notion that America should and would have its day still existed; the Stars and Stripes was obviously a flag of destiny. Certain academicians tried to let the flag do the work, and relied on Iowa farms or Missouri customs to bring in a

city of marble. The others usually felt they could import from Paris – which was really no-place, being only an accepting center of cosmopolitans – the secrets of insight. Then, being American, they would inaugurate the twentieth-century renaissance.

However, as the small group of Americans did discover what had been going on in France, and made themselves a part of it, the concept of a native renaissance died. Nationalism was refuted and the possibilities of entering into a tradition, and working from it rather than on it, were opened. In finding themselves as painters, such men as Stuart Davis and Arthur B. Carles had to burn the passports to Parnassus which the eighteenth century had so hopefully – and naïvely – issued.

The country itself, and especially its cultural center, New York City, also took part in this gradual realization. To the fact of unlimited opportunity had been added the fact of the depression – Hoovervilles and the limited ambition of trade-unionism. Government-supported arts programs encouraged a camaraderie of work and of ideas. Although it has become synonymous with a rather dreary social-realist style and elephantine post-office allegories, the W.P.A. also included most of the abstract painters. Among its members, later to be discussed in this book, were Willem de Kooning, Arshile Gorky, Jackson Pollock, Ad Reinhardt, James Brooks, Balcomb Greene, and Adolph Gottlieb. It was a time when styles and friendships were formed, when parties and arguments lasted all night. The artists created a group of tenuous communities, many of which continue to flourish.

Incalculable enrichment of America's culture came with Hitler's expulsion of the European intelligentsia – Einstein is the patron saint of the most amazing exodus of history. Europe may have resented the industrialized American dream,

Abstract painting

with its standardized gum-chewers, but it abandoned this position as truncheons started to swing. Since 1933, and especially during the years of World War II, among the more recent residents of New York and environs have been: Léger, Mondrian, Chagall, Max Ernst, George Grosz, Marcel Duchamp, André Masson, Yves Tanguy, Leonid and his brother Berman, Tchelitchew, Dali, Lyonel Feininger, Kurt Seligmann, Matta, Helion; sculptors Lipchitz, Gabo, and Zadkine; architects Mies van der Rohe and Frederick Keisler. Some came after the first threats of the Nazis, others escaped at the last second – like the strange and wonderful consignments of Surrealism Peggy Guggenheim escorted to New York. A few, like the late Max Beckmann, could emigrate only after the liberation. All directions, from the whites of Mondrian to the planned daydreams of Dali, were represented. Such writers as André Breton and Nicolas Calas applied their interpretive apparatus to the local scene; Mrs. Theo van Doesburg brought over a large part of her husband's œuvre, as did Mrs. Lovis Corinth. Collectors, like Jakob Goldschmidt; dealers, like Paul Rosenberg; entire faculties of art historians; coteries; connoisseurs – all seemed to bring the cultural matrix of Europe bodily with them. And the great instructors taught – Moholy-Nagy had his Bauhaus enthusiasm sparkling in Chicago; William Hayter stimulated as much excitement in the intaglio mediums in New York as he ever had in Paris, and his Atelier 17 inspired productive movements in the Midwest and West; Josef Albers, Hans Hofmann, and Amédée Ozenfant are popular American teachers; Gropius, who had headed the Bauhaus, is at Harvard.

After the war, some returned as soon as transportation could be arranged; many others remained to become a permanent part of the American scene; a few are still drifting uncertainly back and forth between the two continents. Still, even if New York had not longed for Internationalism, it was thrust upon it by Europe.

The city, in fact the whole country, despite the fright of our politicians, was more than prepared. Polyglot New York accepted the invasion with enthusiasm – despite some inevitable unpleasantnesses while waiting for a Madison Avenue bus on a rainy day, or during conferences with the hierarchy of official culture. There was an interlude when both the guests and the hosts treated each other as spoilt children who had been pampered into various habits of insularity. But soon cliques and apprehensive alliances relaxed and expanded in their secure corners. Newer American collectors got over the shock of finding that big names had tangible owners, and that a Lipchitz was still good sculpture even though the artist worked on Twenty-third Street. Critics stopped jumping nervously whenever a figure they had pigeonholed in history walked in through the front door, and museum officials were willing to include these resident non-citizens in their annual surveys of American painting – much to the benefit of the exhibitions.

Finally, as if to set a seal of recognition on the whole process, the United Nations building shot up by the East River – a marble emblem of a world's meeting in New York, and of the city becoming a point at which all attitudes are taken.

However there is no cause for civic pride.

In Paris the bourgeoisie had a set, tormenting role, which cued even as it attacked the artist. In New York, and throughout America, painter and poet find no such advantageous foil. A mood of aggressive indifference – to paraphrase Cyril Connolly's epithet – radiates from the public. The notion of success undermines all gallantry; an almost irresistible nostalgia (cheerful log-cabins, innocent rabbit hunts) and sentimentality (railroad whistles in the night, *Old Paint,* Penrod) keep the trivial and the clever in demand, and makes creative expression suspect. A park commissioner who loathes all contemporary culture with a cold, active fury, is an appropriate homologue of the New York Medici. Measure success in yards of concrete; when gracefulness is needed, borrow it from Georgian England or Napoleonic France, because grace comes from sentiment – which is visualized in souvenirs from the past.

Except for an extremely small sympathetic group, continually transversed by swift lion-hunters and interior decorators, the artist must be satisfied with constant, active misunderstanding and reproof – from friend as well as foe. He may exhibit for years and never sell a single watercolor. With understandable bewilderment he watches the sensationalist, with a tinseled bag of tricks, make quick profits. In comic strips, the Congressional Record, newspaper editorials, even in articles signed by the head of America's greatest museum, he finds statements of hatred for everything to which he has dedicated his life. Stuart Davis once remarked that it may be wonderful to be Picasso in Paris, but what would it be like in some little town in Illinois where everyone thought you were crazy? . . . In many ways New York is that little town.

Yet the heritage of Paris is palpable in crowded Greenwich Village rooms, in galleries that line Fifty-Seventh Street, in the big old studios on the West Side or in the Forties, where doors were made extraordinarily tall to accommodate the projects of ambitious painters. In cafeterias, bars, lofts and museum lobbies, a cheerful optimism as far as the future is concerned, a self-reliant re-examination of the past, and an assertive enjoyment of the present is proclaimed in painters' conversations and gestures.

There is a feeling of arrival and an ability to cope with crises.

As will be seen, a certain facile acceptance of avant-gardism, a muzzy reliance on a style's direction instead of its articulation, an overly-sympathetic appreciation of personal conceits, are among the unfamiliar traps for new cosmopolitans, and several have found themselves embarrassingly entangled. Furthermore, this is not a New York affair, and painters from Boston to Seattle have added to the new vitality. Nevertheless, the big city becomes the background – New York becomes Paris for the art of its time, and also takes over Paris' tradition. In New York the year's work is exhibited; debates, staged or spontaneous, are loudest; levels of production, most sustained. There is no "New York School" of the 1950's, for the action of the background is that it releases, instead of imposing. Skyscrapers and tenements are different for each and crucial to none. The place is where things meet and happen, where each is on his own, but in a company, somehow – no matter how ephemeral or changing the members of that company may be.

There is no renaissance, no school, no banners to intimidate the visitors from Chicago or San Francisco – for they will feel quickly at home. Despite the efforts of certain promoters, ambitious for some *coup-d'état,* there is no leadership. There is work being done.

The crisis for van Gogh and Soutine was to find a way to affirm the existence of secret anguish and ecstasy, but to do so as creative artists; this, they felt, demanded working in Paris' tradition of disinterested, pictorial means. Paris had its sensations, which were elevated to supreme embodiments in pigment. But its ideal of harmony, and, perhaps, the confident genius with which it gave physical substance to emotion, must have been suffocating to these pioneer Expressionists.

Abstract painting

As has been suggested, their solution was a passionate and totally sensitized identification of the subject with the creative act – emotion became realized in paint as it was objectified in nature. Willem de Kooning's experience with the seductions of "pure means" is probably greater than was van Gogh's or Soutine's, not only because he is a more "professional" painter than they were – which guarantees him nothing – but also, coming later on the scene, he finds pure means exploited with astonishing virtuosity and invention by the many artists who continue to use certain Non-Objective and Cubist idioms. De Kooning's solution has been to make the crisis itself the hero of his art.

Van Gogh's and Soutine's gambles, though triumphant and tragic, were made with relatively simple styles – evident from both the size of their production and the frequent success with which their pictures are faked. In refusing to deny any possibilities of interpretation or expression, de Kooning pays the price of working with one of the most awesomely complicated of modern techniques.

Van Gogh, the paranoiac genius, focussed on a narrow channel, through which everything would come; de Kooning destroys all constrictions of inspiration and insists that the circle of the visual horizon be seen from his position – from such absolutely associative forms as the letter "Z" or a human face to the unnameable white area.

Few painters are better equipped for such a battle with form than this Dutch-born New Yorker. In 1916, at the age of twelve, he was apprenticed to a large firm of decorators and designers (which produced window displays, advertisements, lettering, etc.) and became a full-time student at the night sessions of the Rotterdam Academy. There eight years were spent working up from the perfect square made free-hand to the most ingenious projects of architectural rendering and anatomical drawing. At twenty, master of all the trade secrets, he was a graduated, certified artist and craftsman.

In Holland, the disastrous cleavage between the Academy and experimental art had not taken place; young students, while they were guided through conventional tasks, were also exposed to current expressions and theories. The *de Stijl* group, with its exhibitions and magazine, was a well-known local phenomenon, and its leaders, Mondrian, van Doesburg, and many other painters, architects, and designers, were heroes of the place. The coiling, vegetal forms of the *Jugendstil* – imported from Germany – offered a convincing antithesis to the abstractionists' geometry, which, in de Kooning's case, would not be soon forgotten. Post-Impressionism, the Fauves, the Cubists also slowly captured the imagination of Rotterdam's artists and professors. Thus, temperamentally as well as manually, de Kooning acquired an unusually efficient set of skills with which to meet the crisis of modern painting.

In 1926 he came to America, and quickly found he could support himself with various odd jobs: first working as a house painter, later for decorators and designers in New Jersey and then New York. A few years after his arrival he made friends with a group of New York abstractionists which included Arshile Gorky and was more or less led by Stuart Davis, because of seniority rather than style. In the early thirties, de Kooning joined the W.P.A. arts project, which permitted him to paint almost full-time. Since then, for over two decades, his reputation has emerged very slowly from an underground fame among fellow artists to his present recognition as one of the foremost painters in this country. It was fitting that his large canvas, *Excavation,* should be the climax to the survey of American abstract painting and sculpture organized by New York's

65 Willem de Kooning

Untiled painting, 1940

66 Willem de Kooning

Figure, 1949

102

Museum of Modern Art in the winter of 1951.

In the untitled picture of 1940 [fig. 65], free-forms and a few geometric indications of space are ordered in a composition reminiscent of lamp globes hanging from a ceiling, with room in the background opening out, as if through curtains, to a back wall. But within this simple structure a new approach to the picture is evident. Unlike a similar ordering of ovoids in a Miró, de Kooning's oppositions of depth to flatness are given an importance and intensity unfamiliar in modern painting for over a century. The hanging shapes, establishing their own foreshortened perspective, rush the eye backward toward the egress and its jutting bands, while the background, with its heavily worked, mural surface, and the tones of the globes themselves, keep referring to the pigment and to its own deliberate fascinations of deft handling. Matisse had predicted comparable strategies in *The Moroccans* of 1916 [fig. 22], but here a new personality is recognized at work; each unit of the picture insistently refuses to surrender either its action through imagined space, or its emphatic adherence to the plane of the surface; either its freedom in a completely bounded, curving contour, or its weight as a matter-filled body. The sense of mystery is not revealed in an exegesis, as was Malevitch's "blackness of the soul," or by such overt actions as Picasso's ironic switching of disguises, but is apprehended from the same effect of meaning compounded with motion that one receives from the floating, earth-rooted battlements of Sassetta. The artist gropes to the razor-edge at which separate sensations mingle, but where they still cling to their own identity.

In de Kooning's recent sketch for a large figure painting [fig. 66], he approaches the razor-edge from the other side. As it is fitted into the visual structure, each component must undergo tests and transformations as if each were a purely geometrical shape; then again, it must be twisted and balanced to invoke the eloquent poetry of the massive figure. Finally it is settled in the form where the widest range of meaning is offered. A finger gesturing toward the left-center will inevitably suggest that direction to the spectator. It is the artist who must justify the impulse; reconcile the associative fragment, which is as easily understood as an exit sign in a theater, with its various formal and metaphorical contributions to the scheme of the work of art. And de Kooning, refusing the possibilities of the provincial solution, takes cognizance of the entire tradition of modern painting. Distortion that fits gesture, that underlines its interior hinging of muscle and bone, must also work as the body of pigment which has equal rights in the total aesthetic effect. In a Cézanne or a Picasso it is a matter of linked unequals in a triumphant harmony. De Kooning rejects inequality in even the most incidental elaborations, and harmony – except there is no blend, but rather a co-existence of forces in his work – must exist at the level of every stroke of brush or push of knife. This is not, of course, to imply that de Kooning is greater than Cézanne or Picasso, for no progress or betterment is involved; rather a new style, a new unification of means and vision, comes into history.

In the earlier picture, shapes become ambiguously interpretable form with only the barest indication of reality. The mystery is kept within the artist's and the spectators' professional world. In the sketch of the seated girl, on the other hand, practically every line and tone can be identified – chair, hands, eyes, window. Yet note, at the top-left, the bending cylinders that seem to shoot light, and the small, windmilling shape on a triangular base. They defy quick verbalization, except by simile. De Kooning might, if pressed, explain where they came from and what

Abstract painting

specific reality still colors their existence in his memory. But such documentation would not be important, for the forms act abstractly, with their own laws, life, and relationship to the seated figure. And here we approach one of de Kooning's major contributions: his ability to give pulse and motion to the unrecognizable, to endow the abstract form with tragedy or laughter, and on its own terms. Kandinsky made such an attempt by banning reality and appealing to music and a mystique of color and interval; de Kooning succeeds by banning nothing.

In the period between the 1940 abstraction and this figure painting, the artist, significantly, made a series of extremely realist portraits of both actual and imagined people, and some fanciful genre scenes. Fascinated by the strange lyricism of Louis LeNain, he translated the seventeenth-century sensibility of Laon into a detached romanticism that sometimes recalls Picasso's Pink Period. LeNain's falling greys that freeze in silver to define a farmer's smock, his solitary musicians and forgotten still-lifes, all found burnt rose and cerulean translations in de Kooning's pictures – many of which were never finished – of ten years ago. In order to capture the crisis, which had drowned the sensation of life within the sensation of paint, the artist proceeded to make the most detailed explorations of the visible world. Hardly any emotion is allowed utterance in these images filled with cool, tough blankness. When the fury of sensation returned, it would tumble the reticent actors into a surging mechanism of fragmentation and re-creation. Still, nothing an artist creates is ever lost, and de Kooning's fragile-boned men and women, with their staring eyes and gently folding hands, inform the splashing impastos and streaking shapes that inhabit his present abstractions.

In the two pictures by the artist which are reproduced here in color, the so-called *Collage* [plate b], 1950, and *Ashville* [plate h], 1949, synthesis is achieved and the crisis is the complete hero. The former is a construction of slices of paintings on paper, thumbtacked together; the latter's title derives from the location where the work was executed. Both are small in size when compared to the six-by-eight foot canvases upon which de Kooning is apt to lavish months of steady work – like *Excavation*. The artist is anything but a slow worker, but will paint and scrape off, re-paint and scrape off, until the effort that would usually yield a whole exhibition has disappeared under the final, accepted skin of the signed picture. A practiced eye, and de Kooning's is one of the best in the business, mercilessly judges every passage, either from up close, where each nuance of texture is inspected, or from a greater distance than the walls of the studio would allow, through the wrong end of a large magnifying lens. Surprisingly, the result is a freshness, even a wildness of touch, as a black enamel line appears to have dripped accidentally into position, and as the knife's feathery passage is revealed beneath solid areas of paint.

Each form will suggest an endless series of associations: a curving arm will become a bird in flight or the edge of a shield or a fraction of a face, and with this continual outpouring of ambiguity de Kooning is able to bring paint and sensation to fullness in equality. His creative process of prolonged addition of meaning and interpretation can be compared with James Joyce's writing of *Finnegans Wake*. At no point will the image finally come to rest. ". . . Rechabites obstain! Clayed sheets, pineshrouded, wake not, walk not! Sigh lento, Morgh!" Where the great Irish poet used allusion of sound and tempo to keep the action of his words in perpetual motion, the New York painter uses color and line. The only finality is when the painting is carried from the studio, to be hung in a gal-

67 Arshile Gorky

Image in Xhorkom, ca. 1936

68 Arshile Gorky

Waterfall, ca. 1943

lery, or in the home of some collector; even then, if the picture ever returns to the artist it may easily re-enter the process of correction and growth, and emerge, a month or so later, entirely changed.

But more important than ambiguity of association is that of form itself. Joyce's words may be variously interpreted at different levels and with the application of different knowledges. But the important ambiguity is that of relationship – of the parts to the whole: "Sigh lento": an operatic cry of silence and a slow sigh, also the final Dada gesture with which a composer indicates how his symphony should be played, and perhaps Silenus . . . every new reading widens the frame of reference. In de Kooning's pictures the small elements, coiling and bending (often with an echo of *Jugendstil* fronds and shells), will vanish as they define larger forms; the light object which was so apparent becomes only the outlining power of its darker neighbor; background becomes foreground, positive changes place with negative, and with all metamorphoses the solid core of structure becomes more and more impressive yet illusive. There is no single skeleton upon which this flesh is laid; we discover a hundred supports, all equally efficient, to a hundred aspects.

The trick effect (for example, the thumbtacks, or the use of stencils to create an "impossible" passage of brush strokes) and the proud gesture toward niceties of surface, reappear appropriately in the art of this expert who always experiments. The modernistic ethics of form and function, which announces to everybody when a girder is behind a wall, or how a picture's background plane is pushed forward, are discarded for the standards of knowledgeable craft and poised emotion. Although, in my opinion, he is creating some of the most important paintings in America, de Kooning is not a strictly avant-garde artist. In

fact, as will be seen, he is backward-looking when compared with much other work – as Cézanne was retrogressive in comparison to Monet, and Picasso, to Braque. Nightmares and daydreams, everyday gestures and tragical thrusts, mocking grins and good-natured laughter, and, most of all, an anguished sense of reality permeate his abstractions. The picture is released from the easel, it needs no wall, it accepts no conventions foreign to itself. It attempts to generate the highest charge of aesthetic impulse. All concepts of space, color, texture, or shape can be adapted to its benefit – except for one, that of elimination of "impure" substances. "Flatness" here will never be achieved by imitating flatness itself, and simply spreading thick color evenly. The crises will inevitably intervene, and when "flatness" is suggested it will be in a momentary reconciliation of an infinity of depths.

The American myth of sacrosanct originality (probably initiated by patent lawyers, but today perpetuated by all retailers, especially art dealers) has made the possibility of derivation more unmentionable than that of venereal disease. Still, it may be to de Kooning's credit that the clues to his many black-and-white pictures are found in Picasso's *Guernica* and Ingres' grisaille *Odalisque* in the Metropolitan Museum. Matisse or Toorop leave souvenirs in a rectangle set-off against a corner, or in a fernlike growth from an edge. But most important, many forces have joined: the free-form, accidental shapes of Arp and Miró; the absolute unrecognizability and uncertain equilibrium of Mondrian; the accessible violence and hooking calligraphy of Soutine; the delight in enigma of Chirico; Picasso's exhibited craftsmanship and pride; many other names and characteristics can be identified in de Kooning's cosmopolitan style. His personality consumes them all, and, for better or worse, produces another event in history. This could be the expres-

Abstract painting

sion of the final atomic explosion, or of the prologue to a century of peace; hindsight may call it doomed, or joyously positive of civilization's perpetuation. We can recognize it as an extension of ourselves in culture, as a source of astonishment and pleasure. But beyond identification and outside history, the pictures of Willem de Kooning will exist as colored areas on which violent, shifting emotions found supple yet controlled expression in structure.

Arshile Gorky is a great legend as well as a painter, and the controversies that have accumulated around his reputation since his death in 1948 have come from his thousands of friends and enemies – all intimates – who refuse to reconcile the colorful personality that they knew with the pictures Gorky produced.

The artist evidently rejoiced in facility, not only as a painter but as a dominator of conversations and a source of independent, felicitously coined ideas. One of his more suspicious colleagues, Joseph Solman, recalls how, after cowing a beginner in abstract painting by his brilliant recitations and theories, he added: "The only difference between us is that I saw those issues of *Cahiers d'Art* [where the latest Picassos and Mirós were published] before you did." Or again, he would confound an earnest Greenwich Village discussion, in which Dali was being taken apart for his meretricious opportunism, by stating: "Dali is a great master; I admire his success." His name (which was really Wostanig Adoyan), the date of his birth (it is still uncertain, but 1904 is close; one sculptor remembers: "Gorky was always older than us around 1935, I was pretty surprised to find him getting younger than me in 1942"), the place of his birth (Hayotz Dzore, Armenia; he preferred to give it as Tiflis), his whole biography was a splendid source for improvisation which could be garnished with poetry and anec-

dote – much of it borrowed quite openly from books he was reading.

Willem de Kooning, who was one of his closest friends – for a while they shared a studio – recalls that Gorky "was willing to be confused, instead of 'knowing it all,' and following one path." After a heated discussion, when Gorky had finally and satisfactorily proved that only one style was left to modern artists, he would go back to the studio, pull out a picture in progress, and set to work – in practically the opposite manner from the one he had championed.

He loved to stimulate others and himself with wheeling words, and, until their echoes finally die, there will be many who see in his paintings only the tall, bearded figure who dominated the dinner-table with his defense of Ingres or Poussin and later took over the living room for a long, solo "Caucasian" dance.

Almost entirely self-taught, and gifted with a hand as dextrous as was his imagination, Gorky looked long at the shapes and spaces of Picasso and Miró. In the thirties he staked out an avant-garde position, which, quite openly, would become Parisian, and which would push even further along the lines Paris had indicated. Early, almost in his student days, he discovered a personal calligraphy, his bended oval that twists off to a point, or the eccentric "8" shape that can be a profile or a vase. Quite openly borrowing a Picasso dish or a Léger circle, he proceeded to build up monstrously thick paintings, some so heavy the painter could barely lift them. One of the most interesting is *Image in Xhorkom* [fig. 67], executed around 1936. Shapes that appear to float freely on the surface were made literally inches thick as, almost obsessively, the artist followed their turns, layer after layer, with pigment-loaded brush. For the first time abstract space – the inch or so that the Cubists played with – was kept in absolute control; it was given physical reality.

69 Arshile Gorky

Diary of a Seducer, 1945

Abstract painting

Here a withdrawing shadow is demonstrably about a half inch behind its brighter neighbor, and the optical effect can be checked by running a hand over the surface. Strange, chalky lavenders; light, acid greens; heavy, reddish mud, Gorky's hues do not give the conventional effect of a colored surface which in turn expresses a colored body. He made color a substance – a reality in abstraction – just as he had solidified space.

Within the limits of such severe honesty, an impressive if rather narrow style was defined. Detractors, especially critics with a keen eye for resemblances which they consider invidious, have been too quick to call a source a crutch. As time goes on, more and more of Gorky, less and less of Picasso is recognized in the early pictures. It takes a few years to spot an unfamiliar flavor.

By the forties, Gorky must have realized that such candid revelations of effects and sources, such an embattled and dogmatic stand at the avant-garde, were confining. Almost immediately color thinned out and form, derived from an infinity of sources – from sketches of nature, early Kandinskys, certain details of favorite old masters – was allowed to elaborate itself across the painting, to refer to an insect, a part of the human anatomy, or a whole landscape. *Waterfall* [fig. 68], with its tumbling tans and scarlets, is no longer cemented to the surface. Some shapes are modelled with the care and easy grace of a fashionable portrait, others open to the canvas, not only revealing the flat surface from which space works, but also establishing a rapid, falling and rising rhythm in the picture. We are invited to take a carefully supervised stroll through the gardens; never too deep in the wall or too far into the room, for the artist's hand is securely clamped to our arm. His other hand, of course, is amiably gesturing at the delightful marvels he has discovered.

A more complicated and profound work, *Diary of a Seducer* [fig. 69], 1945, reveals how rapidly Gorky found full eloquence in his final style. One of the most perceptive writers on modern art, Elaine de Kooning, has pointed out how the artist adapted certain passages from a painting by Jacques-Louis David in this work, evolving a whole intricate play of reference within powdery lights and smudged blacks and greys.* Tight, hooking contours are mysteriously animated, often to act out frankly sexual dramas in their aggressive and receptive roles. The tapestry-like decoration of *Waterfall* has been tightened in a more deliberate and confident play of tone and line. As in T. S. Eliot's verse, immense cultivation is felt at work upon an exposed sensitivity, and with similar effects – we apprehend a wounded but mocking sophistication and a certain hothouse perfume and torpor, which are not invariably pleasant.

Because he died by suicide after a series of catastrophes in his private life – among them cancer and an automobile accident which resulted in temporary paralysis of his painting arm – it has been easy to read tragedy into the somber aspects of Gorky's art. In his last works, moreover, a loosening up of surface and an even more inventive formal imagination are seen – so his death was a tragedy for modern painting, almost as much as it was for his own mind. Still, the joyous, affirmative emblems and hues of *The Betrothal II* [plate a] are also typical of the late style.

Despite his delight in a friendship with the Surrealists, Gorky is anything but a literary painter, or even a painter of moods. *Betrothal I* would appear almost identical with the second version in a black-and-white reproduction, but the colors are entirely different, and its heavy

*
Gorky: Painter of His Own Legend by Elaine de Kooning;
Art News, January, 1951.

greens and reds might suggest gloomy prophecy to those who judge by how a painter lived or died. But the problem was to animate form and hue into symbols which could be interpreted as they interact. As in de Kooning, and as in so much contemporary American painting, the lines of abstract, Expressionist, and fantastic art join, so that geometry can bloom like an unknown flower. Note in *Betrothal II* how the pale forms move in perspective against the sulfurous background, and how darks at the bottom supply a rough working platform. But background cuts out the edges, and moves up with, and even in front of them, becoming a new element of fantasy even as it fulfills its pictorial role.

Compared with de Kooning's, Gorky's pictures are at once more subjective in their investigation of symbols and equivalents for human action, and more objective in their detached, almost nonchalant display of craft. Perhaps just because he was so facile a technician, Gorky was often insensitive to the manner in which his poetry was given form. Or perhaps, after the years of fighting with great depths of pigment, he allowed himself to enjoy the freedom and grace with which he could clothe a contour in luxurious color – and sometimes abandon color altogether to work only with grey tones rubbed into the pores of canvas or paper. Somehow he avoided the peaks from where all things are visible, but he went high and far enough to discover a whole world of magnificent fables and jewels within a flower or beside a brook. In leaving the avant-garde of his present, in returning to more conventional dispositions of hue and texture, Gorky made his backward gesture to the past. It was not only a method and a passion, but also a means of advancing, not in relation to his contemporaries – he did not progress from Miró or Mondrian – but from tradition to the future.

Despite their careful preparations and detailed studies of nature, fundamentally de Kooning and Gorky went from abstract forms – perceived in the manifold idioms of Parisian styles – to intricate, human, and universalized statements. Jack Tworkov, whose paintings in many respects resemble theirs, finds his point of departure in the experience of nature, and from there proceeds to abstraction. Born in Biala, Poland, Tworkov arrived in America in 1913, went to high school in New York and briefly attended Columbia University. Like Gorky, he is mainly self-taught, but, unlike the fiery Armenian, he has gone through a steady development parallel to the international abstract styles – working through a rather bland realist technique, through Cubism (Tworkov was influenced by Knaths in Provincetown), to his present, tightly controlled and personal extension of Expressionism.

A tree has burst into bloom against a dusty green forest in *Flowering White* [fig. 70], 1949, a picture executed in front of the subject on a summer day in Virginia. The knitted, hooking curves of black, sometimes describing colored areas, sometimes slicing through them, are reminiscent of de Kooning's calligraphy (the New York studios of the two painters abut), but Tworkov's violent linearity and streaks of pigment are more akin to Soutine's identification with the subject than to de Kooning's refusal to give any part a name. Unlike the earlier Expressionist, however, Tworkov has found he need not sacrifice style – his individual manner of supervising technique. At any point the conscious artist can intervene between picture and sensation; no matter how violently a patch of white will wheel and explode, pouring a river of liquid petals across the image, Tworkov is there, with swift armatures and softly adjusted dark values, to control the structure. In *Green Landscape* [fig. 71], the muscular impact of creation is even more emphasized. Tree branches and trunks, winding paths, sun-

Abstract painting

light barely scattering through the woods, all are exorcised from the painting even as they lend their character to it. Literally *ab*stracting, going towards his individual conception of the picture from the motif, Tworkov almost recaptures an ordered, classically balanced vision of nature. The turbulence of the surface, ironically, reinforces the final serenity of the image (as it does in many of Soutine's later pictures). Colors and lines so intermesh that eventually their tangling smothers initially apprehended shock. Exquisitely balanced and sensitively predicted abstraction triumphs over the forest. The final metaphor refers to the construction of the image, and, after a few minutes, delight in Tworkov's landscape is in his painting.

Yet things are not quite so simple, and there is no finality. As in de Kooning's pictures, here a moment of poise almost invariably will be followed by a push off-balance – then the violence returns, bringing with it, in an inspired rush, the forest and the sunlight and the hand of the artist swiftly and impulsively tearing them into forms.

The statements of a de Kooning are public, ambitious, meant to carry impact. Although they have none of the propaganda shock-appeal and urge to appear strong and hairy-chested that characterizes many eclectic blends of Expressionism with abstractionism, they remain outgoing forces that are bound to impress and influence. Lee Gatch's pictures are modest, in proportion as well as effect; they are intimate, in-gathering, meant to suggest and tantalize. Like Tworkov, Gatch starts from nature, but from a recollection rather than a sensation; he will delve into the visual world with abstraction rather than attack the picture directly, in front of the motif. Born in 1902 of a distinguished Maryland family, Gatch worked in Paris under Lhote and Kisling and went from a streamlined type of realism (somewhat related to the "Immaculate" style of Demuth, Sheeler, and Spencer in the late twenties), through his own versions of Expressionism and Cubism, to the very private world of invention that he explores from his studio in Lambertville, New Jersey. In a way he is a part of the local New York art world, where he has exhibited regularly since 1925 and where he has many connections among his fellow painters. But then again, he does belong in the old stone house, near the woods, fences, shorelines, and gardens of his ancestors. When requested for a statement on *The Flame* [plate k]* the artist wrote: "The inspiration for the picture was the sharply triangulated façade of a stone quarry in New Jersey. Its dramatic height and plunge, as I saw it at twilight from the Pennsylvania side of the Delaware River, suggested to me a Calvary. I put down some notes and a sketch of the quarry and later developed the theme of the Crucifixion in my studio.

"I tried to treat the subject as abstractly as possible and to integrate the still-life and the three crosses, using the central shaft of the quarry as a pole or axle. The effect is that of a double helicopter, one at the top and one at the bottom. This resulted in treating the shadows and the table not so much as natural phenomena but as objective shapes, vastly intensified and extended to create the desired radiation. It also brought about the interpretation of the lamp chimney as a member of the same galaxy of radiating beams, but thrusting up and forming a repetition of the central pole.

"I chose the title, *The Flame,* in almost the same semi-abstract mood that I conceived the crosses, as a spiritual indirection to suggest Christ by a symbol, not by a name or a word, because I wanted to avoid too great a reality in so unreal an hour."

*
By the University of Illinois, which included the picture in its 1951 survey of contemporary American painting.

i Adolph Gottlieb

Romanesque Façade, 1949

113

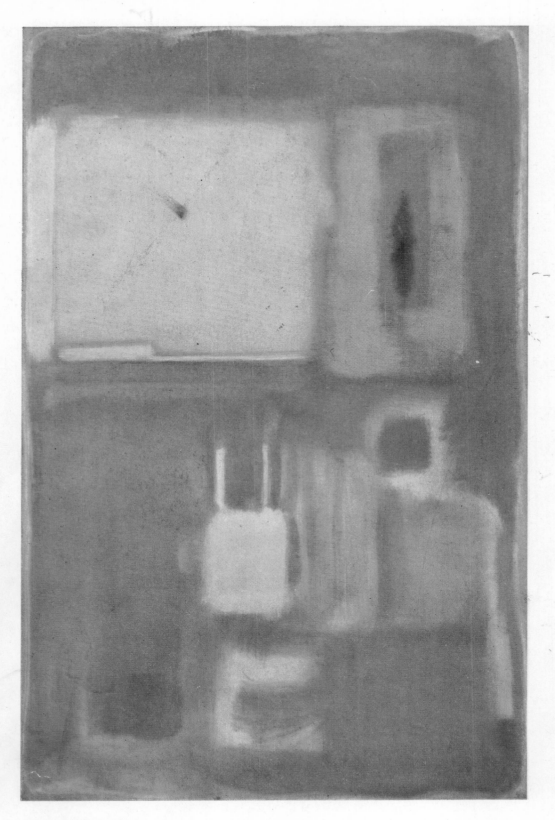

j Mark Rothko

Number 14, 1949

114

k Lee Gatch

The Flame, 1950

115

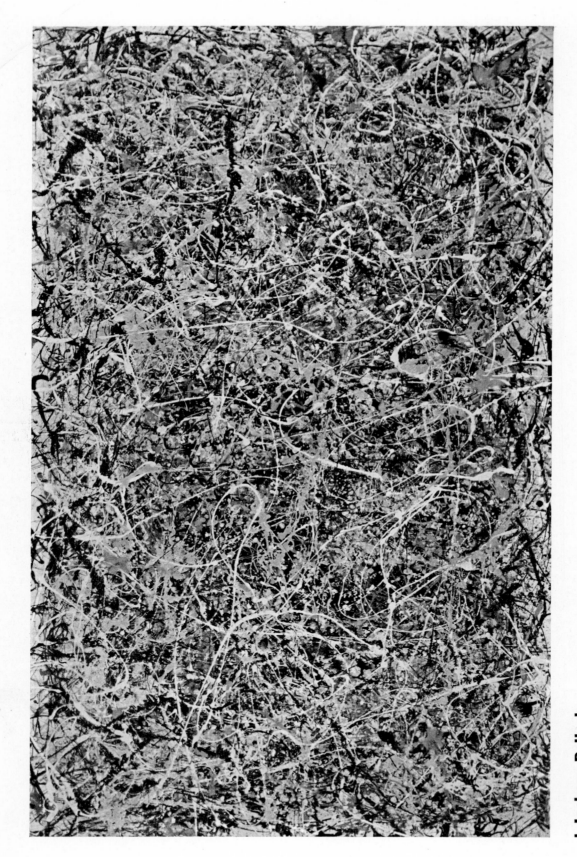

I Jackson Pollock

Number 1, 1949

The artist can name every part of his picture – the lemon, the teapot, the bottles, the doorknob, and every form or plane, and not only in *The Flame,* but also in *August* [fig. 72]. But even after they are identified (and how many shapes can the reader call off in *August?*), Gatch's compositions invariably revert to verbally dumb but pictorially eloquent units in a shimmering panorama. The ambiguity of shape, except for a few clues, is secret; the action of form, which embraces all content, is in the nuance which lets a pine become a triangle of green and then turn upside down in orange. Possibly Gatch finds his nature in abstraction not so much because the time is out-of-joint for names, but because only in abstraction can these landscapes grow.

An architect recently inveighed against modern painters because he felt they had secrets; that they painted wonderful pictures, but no one could understand them unless he belonged to some little coterie. Only then would the snobbish artist unbend and let one in on meanings and effects. Once initiated, he claimed, the spectator could enjoy the picture. Until the keys were given, he must stay outside modern art.

Gatch, even though he is one of the very few painters who actually have anything to divulge along such lines, disproves this widespread misconception. Through weeks of labor – this artist keeps only one work going at a time – the feeling of the picture is settled into the feeling of the remembered shape, or the sketch, or another element which either had suggested. Finally, when the artist's problem is solved, the very departure from reality is more important than any return to it by a cataloguing of sections. The quarry and the still-life of *The Flame,* or star-lit *August,* hold together with the tension that Gatch set up as he went away from a bush or a cloud. Shortly after each passage is named for us by the artist, identification will be largely forgotten, and the

painting quietly insist upon its intimate lyricism between invention and recreation. There is no secret or coterie; there is the fragile adjustment of nature with tone and hue, of angle and curve, which will result in a reticent, involved, dusty-surfaced image. In her sensitive appreciation of Gatch's style, Dorothy Seckler quoted the artist as saying: "Sometimes the only solution to a problem is through a miraculous virtuosity."* The quarry in New Jersey, the lamp, the open field, all may be left behind as the painter surrenders to intuition – which is to say to experience, to knowledge, and even to tradition. This is the only secret there is to divulge, and it has been an open one since the beginning of art history.

Gatch might insist on nature for he has brought a pantheist religiosity back to painting in his infinitely delicate regulations and inspirations. Tworkov might insist on the picture, and with equal justification. At opposite extremes, both have picked up the tradition that goes back to and beyond Impressionism and have discovered that it is a growing part of their art.

Hyman Bloom is usually neglected in surveys of contemporary American abstract painting, and with some reason, for this thirty-eight-year-old Bostonian is usually preoccupied with a merciless presentation of a serene world of horrors. Unknown corpses putrefy before our eyes; a white-sleeved arm approaches the suppurating cheek of a hospital patient; or medical students' hands work, gently as kittens, around a flayed body. Unworried and unnamed, the physical matter of death goes about its business, and Bloom, quite rightly, discloses that such business is a vital part of the contemporary consciousness. In some other pictures, old men in the ornate costumes of Hebraic ritual are encrusted with shimmering clots

*
Gatch Paints a Picture by Dorothy Seckler; *Art News,* January, 1951.

of pigment, which often lend a burning vehemence to their passive faces; or chandeliers and Christmas trees fall like massive skyrockets across adhesive yellows and reds. But while working at these soberly moral statements, which receive their full measure of ethic from the artist's aesthetic position, and remaining faithful to his twin tasks of less-than-human eternity and more-than-human death, Bloom has also created a small group of abstractions. Elaborate ventures are made away from objects as they exist in the spectator's nature, and the conception of the interior dynamics of the picture is independent of conventional space. *The Stone* [fig. 73], 1947, and *Archaeological Treasure* [plate e], 1945, can be read as metaphysical demonstrations of life in no-life, and unexpected birth in waste lands. But when similes become so coherently and completely clothed in their actual material of sticky paint, rubbed and wiped, glazed and pushed on canvas, then the image works both ways. In her article on Bloom, Elaine de Kooning has pointed out how he transmutes flesh to metal, and metal to flesh, all within the coppery, beaten skin of the pigment.* Finally the abstraction becomes as enriched as the idea.

This artist usually brings his paintings along in batches, finishing about a dozen in two years, and the slow process of work, rest, and re-work, gives many of his pictures, especially the abstractions, an independent, self-fulfilled air, like objects discovered full-grown in nature – a curious echo of Arp's laughter heard in the sober, refined art of this Latvian-born, Puritan prodigy.

In *Archaeological Treasure,* the wealth turned up in some viscous soil glitters as if much of its value came from contact with glorifying decay; *The Stone,* pried open like a wound, also presents an interior anatomy of growth in death. Yet in

*

Hyman Bloom Paints a Picture by Elaine de Kooning; *Art News,* January, 1950.

so exactly attuning the symbol with his means, Bloom's minerals are also those of the chemistry of paint. His pure Expressionist style increases its range even as it abandons its usual subject matter

Paul Klee found a springboard to his own fanciful world of abstraction from close-up, detail views of hidden nature – and one could mention in this context such younger Americans as Stamos and Reuben Tam. But Bloom's abstractions are important precisely because they do not seek points of departure, or stimuli. Rather, they arrive at the crusted, everchanging surface; at the upward-piling and quietly toppling rotation of planes and extended hues, by probing in through the stone, or the archaeological treasure.

Bloom, Gatch, and, perhaps, several other painters discussed here, might strenuously deny that they are abstractionists; claiming no kinship with Mondrian, or Jackson Pollock. Gatch, in his University of Illinois statement, significantly hedges with the term "semi-abstract" for a pictorial process that has little to do with representation of environment or the emotion it publicly evokes. Bloom's many realist pictures – although their creation inevitably entails generalization of observed detail and heightening of plastic effect – usually place him securely along Soutine's path, or the early Kokoschka's. But even if Gatch and Bloom owe a considerable debt to the Cubists' idea of a picture, more important is their bringing to form the intensity and the knotted feeling of urgent, named emotion, and loosing it within inventions of paint. In Hyman Bloom America has another artist who fuses the abstract and Expressionist traditions, and who has achieved this difficult act within the limits of his personal metaphor – never forgetting that life and death – the body that relaxes from worship and the one that rests on the dissecting table – are one.

Bloom, the precocious artist and student who,

70 Jack Tworkov

Flowering White, 1949

71 Jack Tworkov

Green Landscape, 1950

at fourteen, could make drawings that would pass for pre-Raphaelite and who burst upon an astonished New York art world in his twenties with a fully developed style, mires his work in slow, arduous labor. Mark Tobey, whose methods are mainly self-taught and who has advanced slowly and with difficulty to his present stature as one of the leaders of the flourishing school of Pacific Northwest painters, makes the paint dance, and delights in the virtuoso turn and twist. Starting out as a painter of nostalgic social-realism, more akin to Wolfe's *Look Homeward, Angel* than to Steinbeck's *In Dubious Battle,* but with the Miltonic aspirations of neither, Tobey proceeded to explore the museums of archaeology which modern art has opened. Deeply impressed by the Orient, toward which Seattle faces, and by Indian and Eskimo forms, he invented a calligraphy which could suspend space within its webbing or move flat-footedly over the paper. In *Structure* [fig. 74], 1946, the tempera lines ricochet back and forth, from color to color, to establish a pocket of light – and in many of his works Tobey inserts little symbols or figures within such containers. By the simple illusion of making the blurred lines appear to establish a conventional background in aerial perspective, and then letting them jig openly across the foreground, he keeps *Structure* as flat as a pressed leaf. Little angles soon evoke their own echoing rhythms, and finally a sense of quiet life is breathed into the emptiness upon which they move, and across their own brittle fabric. Without appealing to any common symbol or familiar shape, the artist invites us into a mystical contemplation of pure action – not for its sake alone, but to realize an almost religious duality of microscopic strength and giant frailty. But the beauty of *Structure* is almost as minor as its parts, perfectly articulated though it and they may be. The flaw here is, perhaps, not so much with Tobey as it is with the

Oriental models to which he is so attached. Understatement to the point of preciosity and restraint to the degree where statement is innocuous – both flaws which so often mar Oriental painting – are evident in this modest tempera. Nonetheless, it points to a meeting place between the abstraction of paint and of idea – and this Wisconsin-born artist has been there many times.

Space Intangibles [plate c], 1949, is a more ambitious work. The cocoon of points and dashes is shredded and spread across the absorbing paper in what at first appears to be a meandering, out-of-focus flow. The magical quality, instead of emanating from the art-school project of a form for space, or a receptacle for light, as in *Structure,* now glitters from a seemingly haphazard disposition of unreadable signs. *Space Intangibles* is a fair title, for this is exactly what happens. Following a coral epsilon or a sandy stain as it changes aspect beneath the veil of blue air, an unconscious order asserts itself. Obviously reference is made to a mysterious communication from some forgotten culture. But soon the message's content makes no difference. Tobey arrives at a philosophical statement of mythic beginnings without embarrassing disclosures of mystique, with only an "intangible" order of space. The abstract picture becomes an involved poetic symbol – a human statement for the mid-century – and still retains its wealth of means and pictorial effects.

Perhaps the note is still minor; perhaps the very demands Tobey makes for metaphysical expression inhibit a fuller range of creativity. But, if minor, the note is true, and its undertones sound in the mind's visual as well as verbal areas of appreciation.

William Baziotes is also concerned with the paint and the symbol, but this Pittsburgh-born artist of Greek descent is far more interested in professionally "good painting" than he is in some state of apprehended godhead. After a thorough training at the National Academy of Design in New York, he proceeded on a search for the forms which would give some meaning to the enormous skill he had acquired.

Baziotes is a natural painter, and in a way a traditional one; I imagine he would be happiest in eighteenth-century Paris, or in Venice around 1520, where grace and beauty could be added to the accepted structure of a Watteau or a Titian, and a painter could work profoundly without having to invent a whole world of ideas. Still Baziotes has done very well in our doomed century, and the optimism of New York may have come to his aid several times.

A series of curves which can angle; an upward-twisting seal-like mass; an oval mottled by darks into stairs or honeycombs – such are some of the basic parts which the artist proceeds to elaborate with remarkable delicacy and ingeniousness. *The Fountain* [fig. 75], a watercolor of 1947, and *The Mummy* [fig. 76], 1950, are basically statements of pure form which trail various reminiscences and arrive at multiplicity of meaning, not by an injection of symbol or object, but by a final balance between the action of a shape and its place in the painting. Baziotes' contours are often as animated as those of Disney characters; they wave to each other; peer upward through green glazes; jump down off ledges; or simply relax on their haunches. How much this is due to stereotyped association – the artist often puts an eye in an oval – and how much to a basic reaction akin to the theories of empathy, is both uncertain and unimportant. In an Arp, there is the danger of sculpture escaping entirely from the artist to run about on a beach – as true and as dull as a pebble. Baziotes' difficulties will come from the opposite direction; he soaks each picture in so much canny painting that it can smother under the sheer weight of elaborate textures and matched tones.

The artist's recent works and many of his early ones have successfully met this problem. The solution involves the most precise adjustments of motion – pictorial with verbal, for they often keep separate identities in Baziotes' œuvre. The activity of paint within the outlines is kept relaxed, and each section of surface is brought to the verge of the "finished" look. Intensity comes from the seizure of a moment before elaboration must stop, and at that time the play of shape within form brings the picture off. In keeping finishing touches off the canvas – which must be a great struggle for this knowing craftsman – Baziotes brings his abstraction to life. Apart from its references to undersea fauna, to flowers or façades, the picture is vitalized as a black line is constricted by deep patinas of hue and by satisfying ridges of texture, but still manages to twist within the body of the pigment.

Adolph Gottlieb's position is somewhat more complicated than Baziotes', although both search for abstract idioms which may be enlarged without reverting to past attitudes. With his friend Mark Rothko, Gottlieb has earnestly sought the place where Mondrian joins Soutine, and where Picasso can be left behind. The implications of this attempt to "become avant-garde" will be discussed at some length in connection with Rothko's pictures; Gottlieb has been content with finding his own explosion of form with sensation, and has never tried to isolate the phenomenon to the point where only the flash and the shock are apparent.

Like Tobey – in fact, like Klee, and even Picasso – this New York-born painter who came to his present style from realist and Expressionist manners, has found in ancient history the shapes that suit his pigments. *Romanesque Façade* [plate i], 1949, and *T* [fig. 77], 1950, are characteristically Gottlieb in their rudimentary division of

72 Lee Gatch

August, 1947

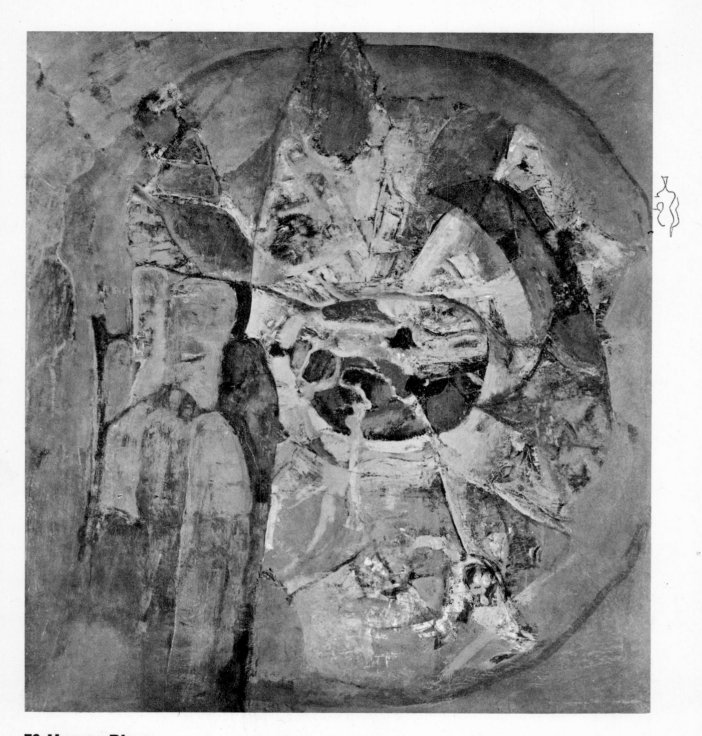

73 Hyman Bloom

The Stone, 1947

124

the composition into elaborate tic-tac-toe compartments – derived from Indian pictographs – and the allotting of unreadable verbs to the various divisions – an eye with two pupils, or six dots, or an arrow, or a three-pronged claw, or a half-moon, or a serpent, etc.

In theory, the idea is quite simple and noble: to re-vitalize form by conceiving of it as a part of magic, or myth, or preconscious knowledge – and thus humanize and deepen the painter's invention.

Paradoxically, Gottlieb has been successful in his attempt even as he has been untrue to the implications of his position.* His early works in this style were prim and dry, like sun-baked clay, and the pictograph was allowed the whole stage for its excitations of vague, subconscious remembrances. More recently, the painter has become the main actor, and, in the two illustrations here, it is interesting to note how "abstract" and anti-myth many of the symbols are – a group of rectangles, a circle, even an empty compartment. With this reduction of symbol has come an enrichment of effects. The canvas is worked at lovingly and long; it acquires the dignity of a time-used object. In *Romanesque Façade,* legendary ancientness is suggested by a display of judicious taste and knowledgeable apportionings of color and texture. The abstract if eclectic "magic," borrowed from museums as facilely as any academician seizes upon a "new" subject, is purified by the labor of love that re-invents it.

There can be nothing spectacular – no moment of crisis or point of impact. Slowly the *Façade* acquires lichened greys and scarlets and, almost humbly, rises to the domain of art. *T,* 1950, in

* Joseph Campbell has pointed out the historical paradox in such painting: nothing could be further from the methods or the products of artists working in cultures concerned with myth than the act of creating myth, or invoking an unnamed response. This, of course, does not affect the possibilities of Gottlieb's picture-making.

angry, greyed pinks and scuffed browns, further suppresses symbol even while introducing a sense of urgency in the torn pigment and scrawled eyes. As always in a Gottlieb, the painting – a "work of art" – is kept sacrosanct, melting to shrewd edges and building up minor, complementing areas of climax whose interaction sustains tension. But now a painter's violence breaks through the pictograph showcase, mocks at the *belle matière* even while stuck within it. Symbols acquire added meaning – one might even call it justification – from the increasingly complicated act that made them, and they refer mainly to it. On such ground, Gottlieb's roughened imagery finds surer footing. In the usually sophisticated deportment of modern art, his archaic, rude mysteries recover their lost charms. The respectable picture-plane is activated as artist and subject meet on even terms, and if the subject is bound to lose (in Gottlieb's case), it still invests the victor with some of its power. The artist has set tension of words against those of form, and his success with the latter brings pictorial reality to the word.

Self-taught as a painter, but widely erudite, Balcomb Greene has had the experience of conducting classes in English literature (at Dartmouth) as well as his current one of teaching art at the Carnegie Institute of Technology in Pittsburgh. As might have been expected, his intellectuality first attracted him to a cool, streamlined abstract style – somewhat like a pictorial equivalent of tubular steel furniture. In the past few years, however, he has attempted to recreate a figure, a gesture, even a conventionalized human action by a process of devouring anatomy with shadows. It is not difficult to recognize the personage in *Waiting Figure* [fig. 78], 1950, although recognition from the painting is not quite so simple as it is from the black-and-white reproduction – Greene's arbitrary uses of color will often conceal

Abstract painting

a head or a wrist. Like Gottlieb, he starts with his subject, but unlike the former's pictographs, Greene's paintings attempt to heighten the figure's real-life drama even as they depart from its lines of force. Light and shade chew into form, sometimes capriciously bringing out a rib or a fold of drapery; sometimes – as if worried by such literalism – cutting flatly through the picture and re-asserting its dominance. To the left of the figure, the background of a room has been pushed out of focus, and the distorting softness of this process almost brutally hardened with heavy, awkward darks. Several silhouettes of the figure are presented simultaneously; not as the Cubists did, but frankly to suggest some sculptured nobility of the stance in space.

There is a certain defiant ugliness in *Waiting Figure,* perhaps a reaction from Greene's long, preceding period of tasteful, flat planes. Disdain for the pretty passage and lush texture is self-consciously expressed as a harsh brush methodically applies rather acid hues in sparse layers. From his aloof and solitary position, which is not without its compensatory drives of anguished violence, the artist patiently twists anatomy to the pose where it acquires eloquence. Thus as far as his content is concerned, Greene is surely no abstractionist – but then neither is Picasso, or de Kooning. In his means, however, he has retained the concepts of freely invented space and color that would put him in this category, as well as his continued refusal to work with the recognizable on its own terms and for its intrinsic meaning and attraction.

More than Gatch or Bloom, Greene avoids categories. His method uses both automatism and intensified planning; his forms are sometimes recognizable and sometimes without identifiable allusion to nature; his statements are sometimes as folksy as a magazine cover; others are totally wordless and concerned mainly with the materials of painting. In holding to this anomalous stand, Greene fights in a picture for what he would eliminate, and often denies entry to elements that might bring logical solutions to its problem: for example, the role of the twisting blacks across the face in *Waiting Figure* or the little flying form at the left. He typifies, and with considerable brilliance of accomplishment, the crucial split between abstract form and human emotion that haunts almost every modern artist.

The painters discussed up to this point have been concerned with introducing natural shapes into abstract styles to increase their range of form, expression, and means. Those that follow also search for such an increase, but usually without attempting to work far beyond the confines of the unrecognizable. The first group might be included in an exhibition of Expressionist painting as well as one of abstractions; the others, although related to the tradition of Expressionism, accept and are accepted in the abstract category.

Best known as a teacher in whose classes enthusiastic students work in rapt communion with well-articulated theories, Hans Hofmann is a leader among younger American painters, and even one or two older ones have attended his courses. His buoyant, sparkling personality, the large number of graduates from his school – they have gone on to work in a wide variety of styles, but because most of them always retain his bold, slapdash manner, their training can be easily identified – and even his long period of silence as a painter, all have helped make him a sort of elder statesman whose influence may be nonexistent on most of the painters discussed here, but whose prestige is considerable.

Born in Weissenberg, Germany, in 1880, Hofmann was in Paris in 1904–14, where he knew the Cubists, Matisse, Delaunay, etc. – a familiarity

126

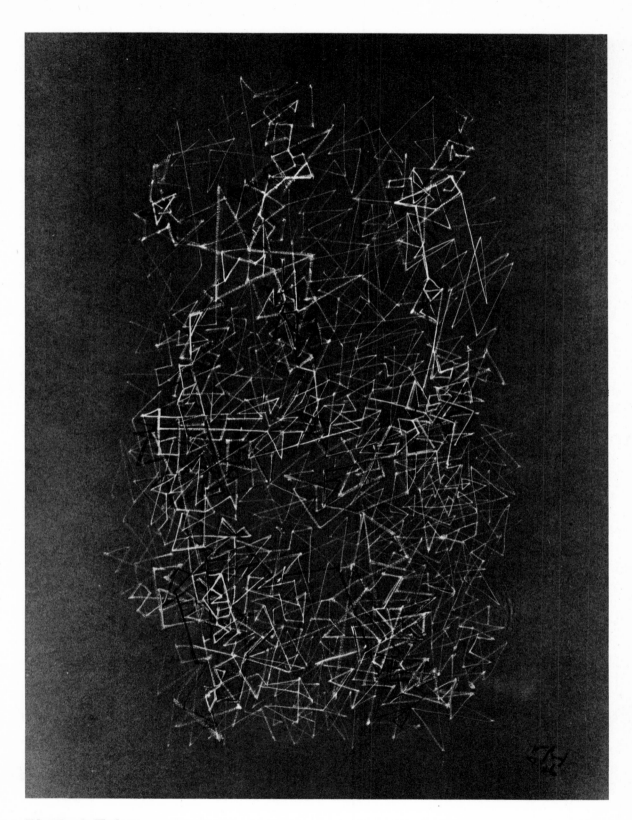

74 Mark Tobey

Structure, 1946, tempera

127

75 William Baziotes

The Fountain, 1947, watercolor

76 William Baziotes

The Mummy, 1950

77 Adolph Gottlieb

T,1950

which has no doubt impressed his students ever since he started teaching in Munich in 1915, and even more in his American school, located in New York and Provincetown since 1934. For many years he devoted himself almost entirely to instructing, but as his popularity increased, and as his classes attracted more and more pupils, Hofmann has found leisure for his own work; since around 1940 he has turned out paintings in prodigious quantity if varying quality. (His classes run on a sort of *ésprit de corps,* a group leadership principle, inspired by the teacher, whose presence is required only intermittently for criticism and supervision on a policy-making level.)

Hofmann paints from nature: from a carefully planned still-life arrangement, a landscape, the interior of a room, a posed model. After a preliminary "warming-up" period, in which he makes colored and black-and-white sketches to suggest an idea for the composition and to practice the supple manual gestures of his craft, he proceeds to the prepared canvas. Colors and forms are suggested at first by the subject, then by the interior demands of the picture, and finally the artist captures to his satisfaction his own sensation of nature within the reference of quite conscious aesthetic standards. Inspiration is stimulated and released to work on the picture itself; the sudden swatch of red which in turn calls up a green across the way is expected to materialize out of the artist's long experience and self-discipline. Hofmann frequently uses the term "empathy," and as he explains the dynamics of one of his compositions, his hands jump from angle to angle – like a fighter pilot describing a dogfight. Abstract form is intended to do the work, and entice the full response from the spectator. The painter is hampered only by physical and intellectual limitations, which, of course, could hardly increase by a change of style.

Such logic, however optimistic and satisfying, may be a little too pat, for when emphasis is put on picture-making, the results may have reference to little outside the four walls of a studio. Hofmann, however, is in no danger of becoming hermetic. *Fairy Tale* [fig. 79], 1944, and *Color Poem* [fig. 80], 1950, come off as images of surging human emotion and technical delight. The former, with its coiling branches, apples, and little birds still identifiable, but strangely mute among spots and streaks of color; the latter without immediate link to nature, have an eloquent balance and intricacy of construction that make an immediate appeal and can reward sustained contemplation. But sometimes, in bringing the picture off so completely, Hofmann smothers it; the process, whose revelation is half the drama, appears unconvincingly simple. One of the artist's more vindictive detractors has said that Hofmann paints a picture like a make-up man puts lipstick, powder, and rouge on a woman's face – doing a complete job of prettification. And the molecule of truth in this libel gives it some significance. Still, if he does exhaust certain works by over-finishing them, Hofmann makes his successful ones among the most powerful and positive today. The old *Improvisation* of Kandinsky becomes a coherent bundle of emotions expertly metamorphosed into pigment. In renouncing subtleties of mood and nuances of reference, Hofmann gets the unified impact that carries from three hundred feet.

Robert Motherwell, one of the youngest painters discussed here (he was born in 1915, in Aberdeen, Washington), is also an influential leader of abstractionists in their twenties and early thirties. Like Hofmann, he believes in the ultimate experience of emotion from pure form, but his ways of seeking this unity are at once more complex and ingenuous.

Abstract painting

Trained in philosophy, art history, and a gifted writer, Motherwell only began painting seriously in the summer of 1941. In a note to the author, he writes: "Don't underestimate the influence of the Surrealist* state of mind on the young American painters in those days, or that, through them, we had a first-hand contact with the School of Paris, and especially its preoccupation with poetry, and its understanding of 'automatism' as a technique; though none of us were much affected by its painting."

Somewhat like Gottlieb, who sought the subject for the desired form, and found his pictograph, Motherwell looked to French painting – Matisse, Picasso, and more recently Dubuffet – for the clue that would allow the poignant human mood to imbue color and shape. He found it in a process of softening and enlarging, in reducing the number of means to achieve more complicated statements with simpler methods.

Perhaps this was the obvious course for an inexperienced painter to choose; surely in avoiding the technical and stylistic intricacies of a Gorky or a de Kooning, Motherwell saved himself considerable time. But he is a natural painter, with a sharp, critical eye for the texture that will bring a color to its fullest intensity, and with a delicate touch at the edges of tone. In the collage of painted papers titled *The Poet* [plate g], 1947, blue and orange – one of the most rudimentary and effective contrasts – and a few indications in black, plus two revelations of the raw paper,* fill the simple curves and angles to make a figure of fastidious monumentality. In *Granada* [fig.

81], 1949, there is no color; black and white ovals and bars are sufficient for metaphor – and this is one of the artist's most successful.

Motherwell has stressed the automatic element in his methods, but he seems to depend more on a process of judicious recognition. Note the battered top of the smallest oval in *Granada;* the use of scratches and streaks in the blacks; or the receptively soft – one might even say tender – edges of the paper in the collage. In such details from a world of lost and shabby images, Motherwell finds his poetry. The *objet-trouvé* of Schwitters is now handmade, and in technicolor, with the final effects of luxurious good taste.

A series of pictures is apt to come from each of this artist's set constellation of shapes; a successful one may precede a group of near-failures, or be its culmination, or be executed somewhere in the chronological center. A leaf, a hat, a torso – usually traceable to Paris – will suggest a suitable scaffolding, and on it the artist will search, with the stimulus of automatism, for the sequence of effects that will release the image into a world of mood and metaphor.

In his many writings and lectures on art, Motherwell sometimes seeks refuge in a twilight lyricism of sensibility – appealing to the autobiographical revelation when a point needs pushing home, or finding a glowing objective corelative to pursuade the reader. In some of his pictures, too, a refusal of commitment at almost the last instant, and substitution of the decorative trick for the pictorial solution, mars the end result. Simplification is also the process of mass-production. But in such works as *The Poet* and *Granada* these very weaknesses become strengths,

---

*
He refers to meeting the many Surrealist émigrés in New York: Motherwell worked for a few months in Kurt Seligmann's studio, and started to paint full-time on a long summer vacation with the Mattas in Mexico. Breton and Duchamp were publishing Surrealist magazines in which abstract painting was given its due as a poetic idiom, and the "official" Surrealist suspicion of formalism was considerably relaxed. Breton even announced the "discovery" of Gorky – in 1945.

*
However, Motherwell does not use the paper as an ambiguous "real-world" fragment, as the Cubists did, but as a differently colored and textured part of the painting. The device is more akin to letting some white paper show in a watercolor than to the pasted newsprint of Picasso and Braque.

132

78 Balcomb Greene

Waiting Figure, 1950

133

79 Hans Hofmann

Fairy Tale, 1944

80 Hans Hofmann

Color Poem, 1950

81 Robert Motherwell

Granada, 1949

add stature to the displayed sensibility and elegance to the final embellishment of structure.

Although he has been painting in New York since 1938, often receiving passing notice for realist landscapes in group exhibitions, Franz Kline did not have his first one man show until 1950 – the year of his fortieth birthday. In a small way – for the art world is tiny – it was a sensation. This mild-mannered, Pennsylvania-born, carefully educated artist filled the gallery with mammoth black-and-white canvases which seemed inevitably "right" and even familiar, although they were also completely new. Like Motherwell, Kline is concerned with the scaffolding, with the proper relationship of relatively few, simple shapes. But unlike the younger painter, Kline's structure is an elaborate invention – self-sufficient pictorially and without need of additional seductions to operate within the largest reference.

Possibly influenced somewhat by de Kooning – especially in his intensification of composition – he has mastered a heavy calligraphy which lends *Cardinal* [fig. 82] and *Chief* [fig. 83], both of 1950, a certain Oriental deftness – in fact, sculptor Isamu Noguchi reports that work along similar lines is being attempted in Japan today. But Kline does not start with the moving brush that writes as it describes. His passive whites are often of equal, if not greater importance than the blacks, for they are only superficially quiescent. It is the white negative – or described forms – that move up and down the layers of *Cardinal,* add weight at the top and dramatic rhythm to the center; while the black, positive – or describing – forms although bearing the slashed imprint of the artist's tools and the urgency of his action, also act as background. In *Chief* the curious insect or aircraft of black dominates, and swinging curves at the bottom and horizontal streaks at the top

focus our attention on the painted form, even though the white area at the left shoots into the image with sure ferocity.

Kline's abstractions are huge in size as well as scale, and he sometimes finds trouble in keeping a simple oval large and still taut over the picture. As in Motherwell's work, a remarkable eye for the exact detail often discovers how to populate empty space. But most often the drama becomes fused to the entire structure. Emotion is concretized by image. Skipping the intermediate step of metaphor, Kline's stable masses of black and white refer directly to the human condition through the spectator's eyes.

James Brooks and Esteban Vicente are highly skilled elaborators of structure who often use elaboration itself as basic material. Brooks, born in St. Louis in 1906, was one of the most successful "American scene" painters in the thirties, becoming attracted to the styles of abstraction after long experience as a muralist – his decorations for the old seaplane base in New York's La Guardia Field are among the more attractive adaptations of anecdotal painting to architecture in America; finished in 1942, they already show a marked preoccupation with non-representational effects. Perhaps because of this experience, Brooks' forms invariably are fitted to the shape of the picture with self-conscious finesse. The tondo, *Number 18* [fig. 84], 1949, works from the outside edge to the turning crosses and circles as nicely as a fine Swiss watch; the blue, grey, and black overlays in *Number 27* [fig. 85], 1950, coil with appropriate familiarity inside the bordering rectangle – like goldfish who know the exact limits of their bowl. But Brooks' restraint is of mood as much as of craft. In order to appeal most directly to the spectator's subconscious recognition and appreciation, he keeps the conscious level – the apprehended and analysed re-

82 Franz Kline

Cardinal, 1950

83 Franz Kline

Chief, 1950

84 James Brooks

Number 18, 1949

lationships – within the limits of muted tone and curbed movement. Diluted washes of pigment in *Number 27* are so completely absorbed by the canvas that the back of the painting is almost a mirror-image of the front – in fact some of Brooks' dimmer webs may have been achieved by painting through from the reverse. Forms, given relative positions in illusory depth by their floating in and out of focus, stay in the weave of the canvas, which, in turn, becomes a window opening on a neatly cultivated landscape of

dreams. Tensions between deep and flat space – as in Léger – as well as the rapid, calligraphic surface action, give a dynamic meaning to this calm, reticent poetry of introspection. When Brooks' pictures come off it is as if a minor miracle had occurred – so much order goes into the mystery, so much withdrawal yields the final, positive statement.

Whether or not our subconscious will recognize, or even be attracted to the images Brooks has found in his art is of no importance. These

85 James Brooks
Number 27, 1950

are not cards for a Rorschach test, although there is no reason why figures or objects should not be sensed within them. Brooks commitment to the order and disorder of the painting has endowed his forms with completeness of statement.

Esteban Vicente, Spanish-born (Segovia, 1906) and Paris-trained, came to New York on a scholarship from Spain shortly before the Franco uprising, which helped decide him to make his home here. Like Brooks', his fairly recent manner of over-all patterning depends upon knowledgeable variation and elaboration of shape and color across the surface, but where the former works with sparse calmness, Vicente relishes the body of pigment in graceful turns of hue and texture. A Parisian sweetness and perfume often breathe from such ambitious works as *Growth* [fig. 86], and *Composition* [fig. 87], both of 1951. The finished look and the difficult passage – green reposing quietly on orange – are as reminiscent of the later Cubist tradition as is the artist's construction in shifting planes. But though he constantly approaches the easily decorative, Vicente's sense of elegance is usually a restraining force. Forms acquire hardness and colors, location as the painter forgets *le bon goût* and attacks the interior motions of figures that melt into landscapes.

Bradley Walker Tomlin is another artist who, like Vicente, finds elegance and taste at the roots of his inspiration. But where the latter builds up details into a final flesh-and-bone unity of image, Tomlin starts with the simplest sort of skeleton and proceeds to deluge it in a flood of dainty swatches and bravura streaks of hue. Vicente's most recent works have been some black-and-white collages of newsprint in which the artist brilliantly complicates his structure with no obtrusion of touch or color. Tomlin, on the other hand, finds his rough cross-frames of support

within the picture less and less necessary, and tends to make the whole action one of embellishment alone.

Born in Syracuse in 1899, Tomlin has made his own steady progress from romantic realism, through a soft, feathery variation on Cubism, to his present manner, developed in the past few years. In the checkerboard scheme of his *Number 7, 1950* [plate f], simple, typographic patterns of white and black on a tan ground set off a few yellow areas and some touches of blue and green with the kind of care – and for similar sparkling effects – that just a few diamonds are displayed on dark velvet in a fashionable jeweler's window. One feels a release to paint in the very freedom from symbol – for Tomlin's ideographs cannot be read and make no sense as "E"s or musical notations, even when these are frankly tossed into the picture. It is not difficult to understand such a sense of liberation, for when untroubled by the constant demand for reconciliation between visual form and its structural and verbal meaning, the painter can give himself up wholly to the refined sensation of paint. In *Number 3, 1949* [fig. 88], – a much smaller picture than *Number 7* – even the simple skeleton of squares is discarded, and shapes float in vague rows on the dark – to all effects non-existent – surface.

The danger here is that the artist's sensation of paint alone may not be particularly interesting; that his inspiration, rejoicing in the beauty of a hue or a passage, may be little but a banal display of fireworks – as emptily virtuoso as the academic painting that attempts to capture pure inspiration by reproducing some touching scene. This Tomlin usually avoids by a skillful juxtaposition of effects which add an amazing variety to his images. The swift fleck of wet paint is even more materialized when its edge is permitted to drip down the picture, which also lends a spontaneous quality – even though its final posi-

86 Esteban Vicente

Growth, 1951

87 Esteban Vicente

Composition, 1951

tion, dripping or dry, was defined only after long scrutiny and judgment of taste. Sometimes taste may dominate, and the results will be little but flashy; usually it is subordinated, used as a tool to gauge when paint finally achieves its most succulent and tantalizing aspect. Then Tomlin's pictures also glow with a joyous knowledge of accomplishment. Craftsman's pride becomes the same thing as the artist's shock of discovery. Delicate, opulent, and with an individual tremor of sensibility, these large pictures are like soundless explosions, and we realize only that there must have been a blast after admiring the intricately descending sparks.

Ad Reinhardt goes even further than Tomlin, and simply lets loose his skyrockets while ardently denying the existence of a "bang." This Buffalo-born (1913) graduate of Columbia University, who is also one of the most witty cartoonists of today, has an uncanny knack for fitting small russet or green shapes together with glints of gold, and letting the whole mass tumble across the canvas like a spectacular waterfall. Larger shapes are apt to cause some trouble, as seen in the untitled painting of 1945 [fig. 89]; although here, by using emptiness as a device, Reinhardt achieves a dramatic starkness – as when the brick back-wall of a theater is used as part of a stage setting. *Number 18, 1950* [fig. 90] represents the Reinhardt waterfall at its best. Without beginning or end, like a section of a Chinese scroll, it offers a minutely decorated surface, covered without particular plan or desire to epitomize any particular feeling; but simply to paint.

There is no liberty of action in such a program, for the artist must keep out of his picture far more than he may let in. In contrast to de Kooning, who insists on attempting to make the work of art omniscient, Reinhardt would pre-

fer to have it know nothing – save its own material presence. It is an ultimate fusion of form with sensation, in which both are denied. Which brings us to the position of the contemporary avant-garde, and the paintings of Mark Rothko.

Reinhardt has, in a way, followed Rothko, as have Tomlin and Gottlieb, in a fairly close association. Born in Russia in 1903, arriving in America ten years later, Rothko attended Yale University briefly, making a brilliant undergraduate record in mathematics. Taking up painting in 1926, he evolved a rugged Expressionist style – dark pictures with twisted heads – which seemed to arrive at a dead end as sensation became at once more refined and complex and form more violent and simple. The first move was to change the form, then, with it, content, until finally a program for uniting the abstraction with the deepest and purest of emotions was adopted. The artist and his friends moved into the avant-garde.

In a joint letter to *The New York Times** Rothko and Gottlieb wrote:

"We feel that our pictures demonstrate our aesthetic beliefs, some of which we, therefore, list:

"1. To us art is an unknown world which can be explored only by those willing to take risks.

"2. This world of the imagination is fancy-free and violently opposed to common sense.

"3. It is our function as artists to make the spectator see the world our way – not his way.

"4. We favor the simple expression of the complex thought. We are for the large shape because it has the impact of the unequivocal. We wish to reassert the picture plane. We are for flat forms because they destroy illusion and reveal truth.

"5. It is a widely accepted notion among painters that it does not matter what one paints as long

*
June 13, 1943; the cause was the "befuddlement" the late critic Edward Alden Jewell was "cordial" enough to express in front of pictures by Gottlieb and Rothko.

Abstract painting

as it is well painted. This is the essence of academism. There is no such thing as good painting about nothing. We assert that the subject is crucial and only that subject-matter is valid which is tragic and timeless. That is why we profess kinship with primitive and archaic art."

In other words, the painters adventure into the unknown, but with some charts, flashlights, and expectations, for they seem to know exactly what they will discover.

Still, the important thing is not the logic, but the position. An avant-garde painter literally must get to the head of the columns, and must fight from this ground. Most dangerous, he must elevate the dignity and glory of the position – which can lead directly to amateurism: any interested, fairly talented student or hobbyist is able to catch the enthusiasm of the front lines, smell the cordite, and proceed to paint or sculpt "avant-garde." Until Impressionism, few artists would have considered gesticulating from aesthetic barricades. Perhaps Monet and Pissarro began it, pushing their ideal to the point where the former, who was by far the greater artist, became involved with paintings which he must have known could not work. The *Haystacks* and *Rouen Cathedral* series are among the first sacrifices of art to avant-garde. Gauguin and Denis, several of the Cubists, many of the Dada and Surrealist artists, the Futurists in Italy, the Russian and German non-objective groups, including the Bauhaus, also helped create an anti-culture atmosphere of program above act; personality above creative expression; ideal above individual.

Transplanted to America, in the ambience of merging traditions from Paris, the temptation to become an "advanced artist" has the same attraction as that of being a success at a party or in business. And because the program has had some poetic, nihilist aspects, it has become extremely easy for the fuzzy-minded and the op-

portunist to accept it. Reinhardt or Tomlin may exclude elements from their painting, and Rothko go even further than they, but such exclusions are creative, in a way additive actions, even if they must result in the sacrifice of a certain amount of energy – as was also true in Monet's case. For the "joiners," there is little but the sounds and harmless fury of a "ready-made revolution."

However, perhaps if America becomes a place where styles are made, it will also be the place where the self-consciously advanced artist will mislead pupils and bore spectators, and it is a small price. Furthermore, as sculptor Philip Pavia has pointed out, the avant-garde performs a certain service in being expendable: "It was sort of interesting," he said, "to see Y's exhibition – I often wondered what such an idea would look like, and I've even thought vaguely of trying it myself; now I'll never have to."

Rothko's paintings are far more complicated than his stated positions, both as to quality and effect – and his position is usually defended in such genially poetic terms that few could take exception.

In his works of the early forties, large vegetable and animal forms emerged from spacious stages to rise in curves up the canvas. *Birth of Cephalopods** [fig. 91], 1945, a somewhat eclectic work, is reminiscent of Gorky in its lyrical animation of details in nature, and one might also mention André Masson as an influence. The French artist, deeply concerned with the magnified glimpse of fields and trees, with lower animal forms, myths, and with taking the Surrealist position while using pictorial means, was working in New York

*

Cephalopoda are the more complicated type of mollusca – squids, cuttlefish, octupuses, ammonites, etc. Their elongated, muscular arms around the front of the head – usually furnished with prehensile suckers or hooks – and their horny jaws, often reminiscent of a parrot's beak, obviously have been taken into account in this painting.

88 Bradley Walker Tomlin

Number 3, 1949

147

89 Ad Reinhardt
Untitled painting, 1945

90 Ad Reinhardt

Number 18, 1950

149

Abstract painting

in 1941–46. But Rothko's sharp awareness of the relationship between large and small shapes; his ability to capitalize on the moment when the obscure form is about to find static definition, and to arrest it in a fluctuating state; and especially his sensitivity to the nuance that will simultaneously make form cohere and disperse its effect throughout the image, all are evident in *Birth of Cephalopods*.

As he pushed his experiments further, empty spaces grew larger, delicate traceries of lines more and more subordinate, until finally the last twig and ligament was eliminated and Rothko hit upon a completely non-figurative construction which is highly original, personal, and which he has been exploiting for the past four years.

Evocation of mood no longer begins with some brief, ritualist appeal to myth; *Number 4, 1948* [fig. 92] and *Number 14, 1949* [plate j] make their rapid and profound effect upon the spectator as independent powers. Thin color has drifted upon the canvas, settling there like fog; edges of hue pass through delicate metamorphoses to spray into neighboring rectangles which throb with angry reds in the center, only to move away again to another exquisitely prepared change of tone or shape. There is a sense of intimacy between painter and picture and spectator and painter – an informality of revelation not unlike that felt in Whistler's misty etchings and pastels of lagoons inhabited by vanishing palaces. But where Whistler's confidences are made at the level of a gentleman friend of the family, Rothko's are blunter, they can be disdainfully vulgar, shrilly outrageous, grandly dramatic. Violence is in color – in pounding scarlets and oranges, or purple gashes into green. The pictures are large – eight feet high is not an unusual dimension in Rothko's œuvre – because, as the artist has explained, he makes a more personal contact with his work when it

envelopes him – and they almost swallow the spectator as well. In depriving the painting of most of its traditional prerogatives and wiles, in reducing it – not to the skeleton, but to the skin – Rothko also enriches it with a directness of emotional statement. Still, impact is seldom aggressive: after the surprise of color, the invitation seems almost dainty; touching in its fusion of color and mood.

Edmund Wilson has compared the artist to Philoctetes – the abandoned, then wooed hero who had the terrible wound, and also the bow of Hercules. Rothko has made his art out of the wound alone. If there is arrogance in his dismissal of culture's history, there is also a humble modesty in his commitment to the very human sensation of the painter at work on his picture.

Jackson Pollock is the best-known painter of this group, and because he has been the most adventurous gambler on the chance of fusing the modern artist's temperament with tradition, he makes an appropriate ending to this brief survey.

Willem de Kooning looks backward and forward, forgetting nothing, eliminating no possibility in the final mystery of violence. Pollock has gone in one direction, always pushing at the extremes, beating at his consciousness for added power and emotion. Both obsessed by search, these artists have brought two new symbols to modern painting: the torn shape that dreams of humanity and the wildly moving line that remembers open fields.

Born in Cody, Wyoming, in 1912, Pollock came to New York at the age of sixteen. Studying at the Art Students League, where Benton was one of the most popular teachers, he learned the flat idiom of American scene realism which the fiery little Missourite was making so famous. And perhaps Pollock did not only learn his craft at the League and from Benton, but also a cer-

91 Mark Rothko
Birth of Cephalopods, 1945

92 Mark Rothko

Number 4, 1948

tain insistence on the strong, virile statement (for the regionalists it was American muscles and guts versus the effete Parisian, with his waxy face and tiny mustache). Benton's veneration of the West and Midwest, of the American countryside, must have struck a responsive chord in the younger painter – Pollock remembers many long trips through the nation in an old Ford and on freight trains.

But if Benton could encourage pleasure in strength and in nature, there was little else he could give Pollock, although the artist now speaks of him gratefully as an ideal source from which to react. From his teacher's sparse temperas, Pollock went to a heavy, dark Expressionist idiom. They say if you starve a baby a bit for the first few weeks of his life, he will have a good appetite for the next few years. This may not apply to young painters, but Pollock, at any rate, has been hungry for paint almost ever since.

After a number of false starts, Pollock, by the early forties, had pushed Expressionist fury and strength of twisted shape and pigment to the degree seen in *Bird Effort* [fig. 93], 1946. Subject matter has become imaginary, and to a large degree suggested by the interior energy of forms themselves; flying wings and beaks lend their action to the title, but there is no attempt to recover the secrets of primary nature. Effort is the painter's and not the bird's. *Eyes in the Heat* [fig. 94], of the same year, abandons subject in nature – that is the direct, recognizable reference – and all that remains is the turbulent process of the artist identifying his painting with himself, and then fighting to bring it out, into the surface of color.

In working on these pictures, Pollock often placed them on the floor to attack the over-all whirlpool of rhythm more directly. Finally the canvas started and remained on its back; the painter gave up the comparatively slow action of the brush applying pigment to the surface for the rapid flow of enamel dripped and thrown, and from this method came the now-familiar style of *Number 1, 1949* [plate e], a work nine feet long, and the smaller *Number 5, 1950* [plate d].

In all four pictures, the artist urges the spectator to join in the paroxysm of creation, in the dizzying spin of the hand and body which will eventually come to rest only as the entire image is grasped and fixed in space. Wings flutter with heavy beat about the bird's emerging head, or a silver line, like a snake of lightning, entangles the whole field of vision. Seeing a Pollock is entering it; one feels like the statuettes inside glass globes that, when shaken, are filled with snow flurries. The picture surrounds one, tumbling skeins of hue everywhere.

After short observation, however, violence is consummated. The image reverts to its enigmatic space on the wall; acquires a cool, almost fragile independence. One is reminded of winter fields criss-crossed by wire fences; of tufts of grass blowing along wide Long Island beaches; of submarine life barely moving on the floor of a frozen, translucent pond. Landscape is interior, not in the sense of within mind or body, but as inside a dark forest on an August day, or inside a lake, or pastures seen while lying flat on one's stomach.*

Pollock's act of strength is also a dream of nature.

There is no finality or repose in either the association or the liberty to associate. The impulse to movement returns; the vertiginous ride always starts again.

*

It is interesting to note that one of Pollock's most recent works was painted on glass, and after it was finished the artist set it up outside his studio in the little village of Springs, Long Island. "The fields and beach looked wonderful through it," he said.

Abstract painting

It has been often observed that there is a relationship to Dada in Pollock's art, but probably this is more a product of the love of strength and feeling strong, with the contempt for weakness implied, than it is an intellectualized aesthetic position. Both Pollock and Max Ernst will shock, and will use shock as an important element in picture-making, but where the Dadaists were ironic, mocking, and self-conscious, Pollock is earnest, obsessed, and introspective. There are numerous gestures of defiance to be noted in both his life and art – he has left cigarette butts and old paint-tube covers embedded in the middle of canvases; in a picture executed in the spring of 1951 he simply slapped paper napkins over strings and wire, and let drawing run over the whole construction. But such actions seem incidental to Pollock's work. He will be feminine and delicate even at his most muscular; work like a horse to weave the daintiest pink and silver pattern; attempt the barest skeleton of calligraphy – green on tan – that would delight a Pater or a Wilde. It becomes meaningless to interpret as Dada an attitude that is so wholly dedicated to paint, even though Pollock does occasionally rebel and pull a strong-arm joke on the beautiful and the pure.

His popularity – although insignificant when compared with that of such standbys as Kroll, Hopper, or even the young E. J. Stevens, Jr. – is not difficult to account for. Encouraged by Peggy Guggenheim, who gave him his first exhibition in her gallery in 1943 and bought many of his pictures, and ardently championed by one of the ablest critics of modern art, Clement Greenberg, who wrote enthusiastically and perceptively of Pollock in *The Nation* and *Partisan Review,* the artist also supplied a specific demand. Not only painters had felt that the separate traditions of abstract painting and Expressionism, that the formal and the fantastic, the contrived and the

automatic, must join. Collectors, connoisseurs, and museum officials also sensed this eventuality, and recognized its fulfillment in a Jackson Pollock.

As the first of the group of New York abstractionists to become a public success, Pollock has had considerable influence on younger painters, in his use of calligraphy and in his insistence on the absolutely spontaneous touch, as well as by his example of glorifying the creative act – a more dangerous concept for the inexperienced. And with such gratifying attentions have come several equally distasteful ones. When conservatives or Marxists wish to point to some real or fancied evil, they almost invariably hit at Pollock. The Soviet art critic and the one writing for *Time* magazine, both covering the 1950 *Biennale* exposition in Venice (which included Marin, Bloom, Gatch, Gorky and de Kooning as well as Pollock), were hunting, respectively, for some particularly horrifying evidence of bourgeois decadence, and for some un-American scrawling. Both found what they sought in Pollock. He is accused of being too fashionable and too obscure, the head of a coterie and minor eccentric, etc., etc. Thus true fame has come to him from his detractors, and his best publicity has been of the wrong kind. This may also help account for his occasional Dada gestures.

Like de Kooning's, Pollock's stature as a major artist seems already defined. The three manners seen in *Bird Effort, Eyes in the Heat,* and the numbered paintings are all mature statements of a creative personality. It would be invidious and unprofitable to compare the two artists' accomplishments, but they stand at the extremes where the spirit of the painter and the body of his paint become indistinguishable.

Drawing learnedly from the past, sensitive to the world about him, the artist in America creates the traditions of the present.

93 Jackson Pollock

Bird Effort, 1946

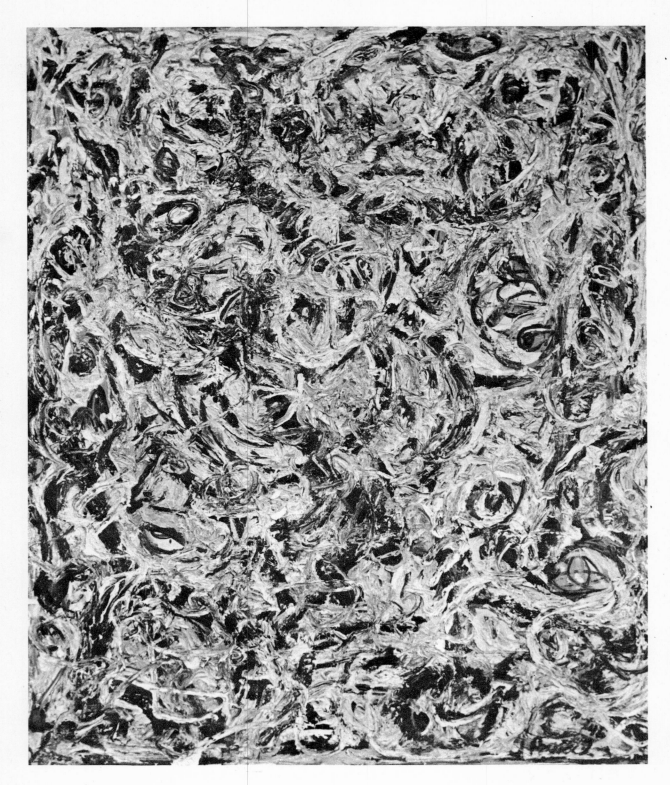

94 Jackson Pollock

Eyes in the Heat, 1946

Afterword

Abstract painting: Background and American phase

The eighteen painters discussed in the preceding pages do not represent the achievement of American art as a whole, or even abstract art in America. Extensions of European styles continue, often brilliantly, as in the non-objective paintings of George Cavallon and the more strictly Mondrianesque (but within those limits extremely original) works by Harry Holtzman and Burgoyne Diller. Carl Holty's recent athletic version of Cubism are also important variations of Continental themes.

Other styles co-exist with abstract ones – although few realist painters concede any validity to the latter. Ben Shahn's hard-boiled nostalgia; Edwin Dickinson's lyrical variations on the theme of perspective; Philip Evergood's skilled allegories; Isabel Bishop's middleclass vignettes filled with sun-struck dust; Morris Graves light-crazed birds; Edward Hopper's dogged apotheosis of middle-class brutality – these, and a handful more, are enriching the varied idioms of local and international realism.

Yet something new in art history, it seems to me, appears with these eighteen painters – not something novel, for almost everyone tried it and many expected it; not a program or a movement, for what marks the success of each is the emergence of a distinct and human individuality – a specific warmth, felt and unique. Rather, in their work a new interpretation of nature and of man is made. Paintings epitomize the sensation of the artist, aware and at work; absorb and reflect it as human inspiration; its mysteries and grandeurs become the heroes.

The pictures have little relationship to the appearances of things in nature, and if it is convenient for us to have labels, then "abstraction" seems proper for them. Space, color, contour, allusion, context – all the multitude of elements that go into form – have different functions, affect us differently here than they do in the world about us, and in poetry based on reference to that world. But the pictures are as living a part of it as we are – perhaps even more, for, as in all art, they are the specific acts that have miraculously embodied the power of the universal. Within this reference, Picasso was right, as usual, when he said:

There is no abstract art.

Color illustrations

Page 5   Arshile Gorky
The Betrothal II, 1947
Whitney Museum of American Art, New York

7   Willem de Kooning
Collage, 1950
Egan Gallery, New York

8   Jackson Pollock
Number 5, 1950
Parsons Gallery, New York

95   Robert Motherwell
The Poet, 1947, collage
Collection Mrs. Samuel M. Kootz, New York

93   Hyman Bloom
Archaeological Treasure, 1945
Collection Edgar Kaufmann, Jr., New York

96   Willem de Kooning
Ashville, 1949
Egan Gallery, New York

6   Mark Tobey
Space Intangibles, 1949, tempera
Willard Gallery, New York

114   Mark Rothko
Number 14, 1949
Parsons Gallery, New York

116   Jackson Pollock
Number 1, 1949
Parsons Gallery, New York

94   Bradley Walker Tomlin
Number 7, 1950
Parsons Gallery, New York

115   Lee Gatch
The Flame, 1950
J. B. Neumann Gallery, New York

113   Adolph Gottlieb
Romanesque Façade, 1949
University of Illinois, Urbana, Ill.

All pictures, unless otherwise described, are oils

Black and white illustrations

Part one

Page 11   Pieter de Hooch
Dutch Courtyard, 1658
Collection the Earl of Stafford
on loan to the National Gallery, London

12   Pieter de Hooch
Dutch Courtyard, 1658-59
National Gallery, London

13   Pieter de Hooch
Courtyard of a Dutch House, 1665
Interior of a Dutch House, ca. 1660
National Gallery, London

14   Second-century A.D. French
Four-headed trophy, stone, Musées d'Aix, Aix

15   Sixteenth-century French
Nailing of Christ to the Cross, detail

17   Twelfth-century French
Capital from the choir of Cluny, The Winds, ca. 1120
Musée de Cluny, Paris

18   William Blake
Brunelleschi of Florence Transformed into a Serpent
ca. 1825, watercolor, Fogg Museum, Cambridge, Mass.

19   Christian Bérard
Acrobat, ca. 1930
Collection Claude Hersent, Paris

20   Jean Jacques Henner
Mary Magdalen at the Tomb of Christ, ca. 1890
Toledo Museum of Art, Toledo, Ohio

21   Quentin Massys
Mary Magdalen, ca. 1510
The Johnson Collection, Philadelphia

22   Pieter Saenredam
Interior of St. Bavo, Haarlem, ca. 1660
National Gallery, London

23   J. Goldsborough Bruff
The Rack, ca. 1845
Collection Mr. O. B. Jennings, New York

24   Albrecht Altdorfer
St. George and the Dragon in a Woody Landscape, 1510
Alte Pinakothek, Munich

25   Fifteenth-century Burgundian
Rock crystal bowl
Kunsthistorisches Museum, Vienna

26   Titian
A Nymph and a Shepherd, ca. 1565, detail
Kunsthistorisches Museum, Vienna

Black and white illustrations

Part two

Page 29   Paul Cézanne
Victor Choquet, 1877
Collection Lord Rothschild, Merton Hall,
Cambridge, England

30   Pablo Picasso
M. Uhde, 1910
Collection Roland Penrose, London

32   Georges Braque
Man with a Guitar, 1911
Museum of Modern Art, New York

34   Marc Chagall
Half-Past Three, 1911
Louise and Walter Arensberg Collection,
Philadelphia Museum, Philadelphia

37   Fernand Léger
The Balcony, 1914
Private collection

39   Henri Matisse
The Moroccans, 1916
Collection the artist, Nice

40   Pablo Picasso
Three Musicians, 1921
Museum of Modern Art, New York

43   Pablo Picasso
Still-life with Guitar, 1913, collage
Collection Sidney Janis, New York

44   Georges Braque
Still-life with Newspaper, 1912, collage
Buchholz Gallery, New York

45   Pablo Picasso
Guitar and Glasses, 1913
A. E. Gallatin Collection
on loan to the Philadelphia Museum, Philadelphia

46   Henri Matisse
Icarus, 1946
pasted paper illustration for the book Jazz

47   George Grosz
The Lighthouse of Bornholm and the Floating
Boatsman, 1932, collage, Collection the artist

48   Kurt Schwitters
Merz, 33, 1920, collage
Private collection

49   Piet Mondrian
Composition in Line, 1913
Rijksmuseum Kroller-Muller, Harskamp, Holland

50   Kasimir Malevich
Suprematist Composition, Two Squares, 1913, drawing
On extended loan to the Museum of Modern Art,
New York

51   Theo van Doesburg
Design for a Stained-Glass Window, 1924, watercolor
Collection Nellie van Doesburg, New York

52   Piet Mondrian
New York, 1942
Private Collection, New York

54   Ben Nicholson
Still-life (Punch and Judy Show), 1932-37
Durlacher Brothers, New York

55   Pablo Picasso
The Red Tablecloth, 1924
Private collection, New York

56   Wassily Kandinsky
Black Lines, 1913
Solomon R. Guggenheim Foundation, New York

57   Jean Arp
Arpaden, 1918-22, drawing for book illustration
Museum of Modern Art, New York

59   Joan Miró
Untitled painting, 1925
Collection Pierre Matisse, New York

60   Pablo Picasso
Project for a Monument, 1928, drawing
Museum of Modern Art, New York

62   Alexander Calder
A New Alphabet of Forms, 1942, drawing
Private collection

Black and white illustrations

64 Vincent van Gogh
    Landscape in the Rain, 1889
    Collection Henry P. McIlhenny, Philadelphia

66 Paul Gauguin
    The Sacred Mountain, 1882
    Collection Mr. and Mrs. Rodolphe de Schauensee,
    Philadelphia

68 Edvard Munch
    White Night, 1901
    National Gallery, Oslo

69 Wassily Kandinsky
    Landscape, 1911
    Solomon R. Guggenheim Foundation, New York

71 Chiam Soutine
    The Hill, ca. 1919
    Collection Sidney Janis, New York

72 Oskar Kokoschka
    The Crab, 1940-1941
    Collection Major Beddington Behrens, London

73 Henri Matisse
    The Terrace, St. Tropez; ca. 1904
    Isabella Stewart Gardner Museum, Boston

75 Pierre Bonnard
    The Riviera, 1928
    Phillips Gallery, Washington, D.C.

76 Paul Gauguin
    Manao Tupapao (Watched by the Spirit of
    the Dead), ca. 1893-95, woodcut
    Art Institute of Chicago, Chicago

77 James Ensor
    Magic Musicians, 1891
    Private collection

78 Giorgio de Chirico
    Disturbing Journey, 1913
    Museum of Modern Art, New York

79 Max Ernst
    The Forest, 1928
    Private collection

80 Paul Klee
    Mask of Fear, 1932
    Collection Dr. Allan Roos, New York

81 Pablo Picasso
    Night Fishing at Antibes, 1939
    Private collection

82 Joseph Stella
    Battle of Light, Coney Island, 1913
    Collection Société Anonyme, Yale University,
    New Haven, Connecticut

83 Morgan Russell
    To Form Synchromy, Number 4, 1914
    Rose Fried Gallery, New York

84 Max Weber
    Rush Hour, New York, 1915
    Collection the Artist, Long Island, New York

85 Stuart Davis
    The President, 1922
    Collection the artist, New York

86 Alfred Maurer
    Still-life with Pears, ca. 1931
    Addison Gallery of American Art, Andover,
    Massachusetts

87 Arthur Dove
    The Brothers, 1941
    The Downtown Gallery, New York

88 Karl Knaths
    The Moon, 1950
    Worcester Art Museum, Worcester, Massachusetts

89 Stuart Davis
    Report from Rockport, 1940
    Collection Mr. and Mrs. Milton Lowenthal, New York

90 Arthur B. Carles
    Turkey, 1927
    Collection the artist, Chestnut Hill, Pennsylvania

91 Arthur B. Carles
    Painting, 1935-40
    Collection the artist, Chestnut Hill, Pennsylvania

Black and white illustrations

Part three

Page 101 Willem de Kooning
Untitled painting, 1940
Collection Walter Auerbach, New York

102 Willem de Kooning
Figure, 1949
Egan Gallery, New York

105 Arshile Gorky
Image in Xhorkom, ca. 1936
Collection Jeanne Reynal, New York

106 Arshile Gorky
Waterfall, ca. 1943
Arshile Gorky Estate, New York

109 Arshile Gorky
Diary of a Seducer, 1945
Collection Julien Levy, Bridgewater, Connecticut

119 Jack Tworkov
Flowering White, 1949
Egan Gallery, New York

120 Jack Tworkov
Green Landscape, 1950
Egan Gallery, New York

123 Lee Gatch
August, 1947
University of Nebraska Art Galleries, Lincoln,
Nebraska

124 Hyman Bloom
The Stone, 1947
Collection Mr. and Mrs. John Makin, Blue Hill,
Maine

127 Mark Tobey
Structure, 1946, tempera
Collection Edward W. Root, Clinton, New York

128 William Baziotes
The Fountain, 1947, watercolor
Kootz Gallery, New York

129 William Baziotes
The Mummy, 1950
Collection Edward W. Root, Clinton, New York

130 Adolph Gottlieb
T, 1950
Kootz Gallery, New York

133 Balcomb Greene
Waiting Figure, 1950
Bertha Schaefer Gallery, New York

134 Hans Hofmann
Fairy Tale, 1944
Kootz Gallery, New York

135 Hans Hofmann
Color Poem, 1950
Kootz Gallery, New York

136 Robert Motherwell
Granada, 1949
Kootz Gallery, New York

138 Franz Kline
Cardinal, 1950
Egan Gallery, New York

139 Franz Kline
Chief, 1950
Egan Gallery, New York

140 James Brooks
Number 18, 1949
Peridot Gallery, New York

141 James Brooks
Number 27, 1950
Peridot Gallery, New York

143 Esteban Vicente
Growth, 1951
Peridot Gallery, New York

144 Esteban Vicente
Composition, 1951
Peridot Gallery, New York

147 Bradley Walker Tomlin
Number 3, 1949
Parsons Gallery, New York

148 Ad Reinhardt
Untitled painting, 1945
Collection the artist, New York

149 Ad Reinhardt
Number 18, 1950
Parsons Gallery, New York

151 Mark Rothko
Birth of Cephalopods, 1945, oil and tempera
Collection the artist, New York

152 Mark Rothko
Number 4, 1948
Parsons Gallery, New York

155 Jackson Pollock
Bird Effort, 1946
Collection the artist, New York

156 Jackson Pollock
Eyes in the Heat, 1946
Collection Peggy Guggenheim, Venice

Acknowledgments

To The Art Foundation, *Art News* magazine, and its Editor, Alfred M. Frankfurter go my sincere thanks for permission to use their extensive files of photographs. Many of the artists discussed here, and their dealers and friends, have submitted to requests for material with unfailing politeness and co-operation and encouragement; without their help this book could not have been written. I am also indebted to Milton Rugoff for his editing; Clement Greenberg, who suggested the idea in the first place; and to Elaine de Kooning, Dorothy Seckler, Philip Pavia, Henri Peyre, Paul Stamm, and Edgar B. Stern for help and advice, even though some of these were unaware it was being applied to this end. Finally to my wife, who has seen the work through from beginning to end, go my deepest expressions of gratitude and appreciation. *January-May, 1951*

This book was designed by Bradbury Thompson

Set in Baskerville and Franklin Gothic types by Norwood Press, Norwood, Mass.
Black and white illustrations and text were printed by the Kipe Offset Process Co., New York
Color illustrations were printed by Ram Press, New York